T0386764

beautiful man
&
other
short
plays

also by erin shields

If We Were Birds
Mistatim / Instant
Paradise Lost
Soliciting Temptation

beautiful man & other short plays

Beautiful Man

Unit B-1717

And then there was you

erin shields

playwrights canada press
toronto

For professional or amateur production rights, please contact:
Ian Arnold at Catalyst TCM
15 Old Primrose Lane, Toronto, ON M5A 4T1
416-568-8673 | ian@catalysttcm.com

LIBRARY AND ARCHIVES CANADA CATALOGUING IN PUBLICATION
Title: Beautiful man : & other short plays / Erin Shields.
Other titles: Plays. Selections (2020)
Names: Shields, Erin, author.
Identifiers: Canadiana (print) 20200386875 | Canadiana (ebook) 20200386921
  | ISBN 9780369101495 (softcover) | ISBN 9780369101501 (PDF)
  | ISBN 9780369101518 (HTML) | ISBN 9780369101525 (Kindle)
Classification: LCC PS8637.H497 A6 2020 | DDC c812/.6—dc23

Playwrights Canada Press operates on Mississaugas of the Credit, Wendat, Anishinaabe, Métis, and Haudenosaunee land. It always was and always will be Indigenous land.

We acknowledge the financial support of the Canada Council for the Arts—which last year invested $153 million to bring the arts to Canadians throughout the country—the Ontario Arts Council (OAC), Ontario Creates, and the Government of Canada for our publishing activities.

For my sisters, Alison, Meghan and Caitlin.

introduction

andrea donaldson

When Erin entered the scene almost twenty years ago, she was stepping into a theatre ecology that preferred and promoted the new plays of cis men—a scene that viewed male protagonists as universal and women protagonists as niche. This pressure has been the fuel for her life's work, energy that is still, twenty years later, relevant and vital. Her work runs deep—always pushing against a system, revising and usurping the words of old masters and breathing freshness into the age-old. The rebel inside of her insists that she push against a world that instructs her to be demure, reserved and a supporting character. But her queerness and womaness infuses the way she thinks, informs her place as outsider, rebel and radical and asserts an undeniable lens and agenda.

Though her earliest works focused on solo storytelling, she was moved to tell stories epic in scope, expressed through large casts. Her ambitiousness, a trait the world has been unable to train out of her, allows her to ask for the space, time and support to dream big, and her own diligence and appetite for the impossible makes sure that each project finds a home. And so Erin swiftly leapt in her career from a self-producing playwright to a writer produced on our nation's largest stages. And yet, true to herself and bound by integrity, she still nimbly hops from the Stratford Festival, to indie site-specific works, to the National Arts Centre and to SummerWorks when the urgency of her work has demanded it.

The three plays in this book are examples of those urgent works that Erin crafted either by invitation or through creative imperative. Of these three works, I directed one—*Beautiful Man*—and have read two: *And then there was you* and *Unit B-1717*. As one of her earliest collaborators, I can feel the pluck and piquancy in these pieces that characterized her thrust onto the scene yet see the devotion to craft that her career has exemplified.

When Erin is asked what moves her to write, she is always quick to answer, "My rage," with a cheeky smile and probably a laugh with her head cocked back. This is certainly true of *Beautiful Man*, a piece that was responding to the violence and misogyny in our daily lives and pop culture, as well as in the many exposures of abuse that were surfacing at that time, seemingly prophesying the #metoo movement.

Part of the lore of *Beautiful Man* is that Erin wrote it almost overnight. In true Shields fashion, she brewed and stewed and then sat down and unleashed the work onto the page. She then caught me on break from rehearsal and, knowing the piece needed to happen immediately to respond to the moment, said, "I think we should do this at SummerWorks." And we did. Subsequently, Factory Theatre came on as a producer for the world premiere, and the piece was workshopped, redrafted and now includes a stunning twenty-minute monologue by Beautiful Man at the end of the piece.

In *Unit B-1717*, Erin again probes the interior world of a woman, this time animating storage containers that were an inciting force in the experiment. We can see how the compartments of our protagonist's mind are echoed in the live environment this work is meant to inhabit. And again we are introduced to the agony of absorbing others' feelings and needs before one's own—a strong feminist throughline in each of these plays.

In *And then there was you*, we are exposed to the interior life of a woman experiencing the intimacy and loss of motherhood. The perspective is eerily authentic, and, once again, Erin uses language to voice the deep unspoken truths of carrying a child, wrangling a toddler and the various stages of letting go required of parenting. She skilfully articulates the pain that women absorb—this time not the microaggressions of male counterparts, but of the appropriately self-centred perspectives and actions of a child transitioning to adulthood. As a director who has only experienced this work on the page, I am invited to imagine this play without a container of stage directions, or directives or gestures toward how it should be seen. Yet I find it no surprise that in its first interpretation it was animated by a small army of fierce female performers versus a single performer as the monologue form would suggest. Erin's blend of the everyday and the profound is rich in this piece and a mainstay of her work, and, as always, her formatting gives clues to actors regarding the lyricism, breath and muscularity required.

When I read these three works, I experience three pieces that invite rich participation and invention from collaborators to propose staging, physicality and sound and to connect with challenging text that, while embracing highly sophisticated theatrical forms, is rooted in poetry. Erin's lust for language fused with her ability to embed complex structure and literary playfulness is astounding. She understands action and language like no other living playwright I know, and the refinement of her craft never compromises the visceral experience of her works, which are meant to grip, seduce, shock and offer release.

These works are poetic, wicked, deliberate and uncanny and expertly reinvent and re-centre power. Erin's ability to use theatre as a method to destabilize power and confront injustice and apathy is apparent in every work she makes. While Erin holds language as one of humanity's most blessed and healing gifts, she simultaneously recognizes language's power to trap, assert and erase. She harnesses language in a fight for liberation, visibility and complexity.

In these works, Erin reveals humanness in all of its truths, examining our beautiful and lesser impulses. She holds herself accountable, which in turn transforms her understanding of the world we live in and reveals us to ourselves. She does not preach to the choir, but, rather, continually asks us if we are good, how we are good and how we are failing each other and ourselves. There is beauty in her interrogations, there is dismantling in her interrogations and there is hope—not through pandering—but through the artistic pulse and appetite for change she ignites in her audiences. Through this we are left enlivened, we are allowed to exist despite the histories that have erased us and we are reminded of our choice to be active accomplices or denouncers of oppressive systems.

It is especially magical to see a writer who, after creating for twenty years, still holds the spark of her younger, rougher self throughout her career. The embers have not grown cold in service of growing works for larger stages and broader audiences, but have rather been stoked to ignite and roar with the expertise that can only come from thousands of hours of writing over two decades and the chance to experience one's plays with audiences again and again.

I am grateful for my fearless friend, whose words invoke beauty, fury and power. And grateful the world has access to this contemporary truth-teller—whether we're ready for her or not.

Andrea Donaldson has directed award-winning productions for theatres across Canada, including Soulpepper, Factory Theatre, Tarragon Theatre, Theatre Passe Muraille, Theatre Direct, the Great Canadian Theatre Company, the Festival Players of Prince Edward County, the National Theatre School, SummerWorks, the St. Lawrence Shakespeare Festival, Shakespeare in the Ruff, Espace René-Provost, the Toronto Fringe, Red Sky Performance and Nightwood Theatre. For two decades Donaldson has played a pivotal role in fostering new feminist works for the stage as a freelance director/dramaturge, in her role as Tarragon's Associate Artistic Director, and at Nightwood Theatre as Program Director of Write from the Hip and now as Artistic Director.

beautiful man

For Andrea Donaldson.
Thank you for continuing to realize my work
with integrity, humour and beauty.

special thanks

Thank you to Nina Lee Aquino and Jonathan Heppner for programming and producing *Beautiful Man*, and to all the artists who contributed to the production. A special thank you to the team of the Groundwater Productions workshop production of *Beautiful Man* at SummerWorks in 2015: Andrea Donaldson, Anusree Roy, Ava Jane Markus, Brett Donahue, Melissa D'Agostino, Jason Hand, Laura Gardner, Richard Feren, Lauren Vandervoort and Sean Miller.

A workshop production of *Beautiful Man* was originally staged at the SummerWorks Festival in 2015. The full production premiered at Factory Theatre, Toronto, from May 4 to 26, 2019, with the following cast and creative team:

Sophie: Mayko Nguyen
Jennifer: Ashley Botting
Pam: Sofia Rodriguez
Beautiful Man: Jesse LaVercombe

Director: Andrea Donaldson
Lighting Design: Jason Hand
Set Design: Gillian Gallow
Sound Design: Richard Feren
Costume Design: Ming Wong
Head of Wardrobe: Chanti Laliberte
Assistant Director: Keshia Palm
Stage Manager: Andrea Baggs
Apprentice Stage Manager: Michaela Steven
Dramaturge: Matt McGeachy
Apprentice Assistant Director: Miquelon Rodriguez

characters

Sophie
Jennifer
Pam
Beautiful Man

setting

Now

part 1

Lights up on three women.
They stand together.
Behind them, and above, stands BEAUTIFUL MAN.
Maybe he stays in one place throughout the play.
Maybe he is constantly in motion.
He is apart from the women.
He is different.
BEAUTIFUL MAN is always well lit, always carefully dressed, always beautiful.
Throughout the play his clothes are removed and he becomes even more beautiful.
Though we can't quite believe it, he grows even more beautiful.

SOPHIE: Did you see that movie?

JENNIFER: Which one?

SOPHIE: You know, that new one.

JENNIFER: That new one with the cops?

SOPHIE: Yes, with the cops, and they're trying to catch this woman.

JENNIFER: A woman who robs banks.

SOPHIE: A woman who takes men.

JENNIFER: Right, a serial killer who takes men.

PAM: Beautiful men, I saw it, yes.

JENNIFER: She's a psychopath.

SOPHIE: Not the cop.

JENNIFER: No, the killer.

PAM: The killer is the psychopath.

SOPHIE: I love the cop, that main cop, what's her name?

PAM: Rosie.

SOPHIE: Rosie, yes, that's it, and she's got some problems.

PAM: Right, she's got issues.

JENNIFER: Demons she can't ignore, so she's a drinker,
been on and off the wagon more times than she can count,
which is why she's got to sneak to do it.

PAM: To drink?

JENNIFER: To drink, that's right, and she needs to drink,
can't help herself, really, because she's got a past.

SOPHIE: A terrible past and she wants to blot it out.

JENNIFER: She needs to blot it out.

PAM: It's that cold case with the kid,
that's the one that really got her.
It haunts her to this day.

JENNIFER: To this day she can still see
his body in that dumpster.

SOPHIE: I thought he was in a bathtub.

PAM: His body in pieces in the trunk of a car.

SOPHIE: But that case, it transformed her.

JENNIFER: Made her the cop she is today,
and now she can't ignore a thing,
can't let a detail drop.

SOPHIE: And this backstory makes you understand
why she's tortured,
why she does the things she does,
and that actor, she really nails it,
she really gets into the part.

PAM: I think she does the Method.

JENNIFER: Yes, I heard she does the Method.

SOPHIE: The Method where she swims across a lake in real life
if her character swims across a lake in a movie?

PAM: I remember that movie where she swam across that lake.

JENNIFER: Yes, her character swam across a lake in that movie
so in real life she swam across a lake.

SOPHIE: A big lake, yes, for that movie.

JENNIFER: What was that movie?

PAM: *Lake Swimmer?* Was that the name?

JENNIFER: *Lake Swimmer*, yes, that's it.

SOPHIE: Yes, that's it, but in this movie she's a cop.

PAM: I wonder if she had to shoot someone to get into this movie?

SOPHIE: She wouldn't have had to shoot someone.

JENNIFER: No, they wouldn't have made her do that.

SOPHIE: Not a person.

JENNIFER: But an animal, maybe.

SOPHIE: Yes, I heard she went out hunting.

JENNIFER: Spent three months in the Yukon
with hunters really hunting.

PAM: But there's no hunting in this movie.

JENNIFER: Yes, there's hunting.

SOPHIE: She's hunting a serial killer.

JENNIFER: That's right, which is more or less the same,
more or less the equivalent of hunting a buck in the woods.

SOPHIE: At least emotionally.

JENNIFER: Emotionally, yes, which is all that's important
to follow the Method, which is why she's so believable
as the serial-killer-hunting cop.

SOPHIE: And there's a boyfriend, right?
Rosie's got a man?

JENNIFER: You're right, she's got a man.

PAM: What's his name?

SOPHIE: I can't remember.

JENNIFER: But he's hot.

SOPHIE: He's smoking hot.

JENNIFER: Tight ass, strong chest, makes you want to slap him.

SOPHIE: Yes, you sort of want to slap him.

PAM: But he's sweet.

SOPHIE: Sure, he's sweet.

JENNIFER: Like you sort of want to lick him.

SOPHIE: Yes, you sort of want to lick him
and you sort of want to slap him
and he wants Rosie to settle down,
but she just can't take the pressure,
she can't commit to the commitment.

PAM: But she knows he's a nice guy.
She knows he's very sweet.

SOPHIE: But that doesn't make it easier.

JENNIFER: In fact, it makes it harder because she can't help
getting obsessed with case after case after case.

SOPHIE: And she can't help but shrug him off when he says things like:

BEAUTIFUL MAN: How was your day?

JENNIFER: Right, it actually makes her angry
when he says stupid things like:

BEAUTIFUL MAN: How was your day?

JENNIFER: It really pisses her off.

BEAUTIFUL MAN: Honey? Are you listening to me?

SOPHIE: Oh it really makes her crazy because if he knew,
if he had any idea what kind of a day
she was still in the middle of having,
he'd know that was a stupid question.

JENNIFER: A ridiculously simple question.

PAM: Because it's been a very hard day, actually.

JENNIFER: Another very hard day in a string of very hard days
and what does he know about it.
He's just a teacher, every day is—

SOPHIE: Is he a teacher?

PAM: I thought he worked in a flower shop.

SOPHIE: I thought he was a nurse.

JENNIFER: A nurse, that's right, he's a nurse.

SOPHIE: In a hospital for sick children,
so she knows he's saving lives.
He's saving the lives of children
while she's counting up the bodies,

which only makes it worse
because she shouldn't really be angry,
she shouldn't take it out on *him*.
He's one of the good ones;
one of the good guys in this world.

PAM: And he smiles at her like he understands.

BEAUTIFUL MAN: It's okay, I understand.

SOPHIE: But he doesn't understand;
he'll never understand.
And that's what really gets her.

JENNIFER: She brushes him aside and pours a glass of whiskey.
She can't stand to look at the look on his face.
If he knew what she'd been through that day,
if he had any idea,
he wouldn't be giving her that look of expectation,
that exasperated look of indignation.

SOPHIE: No, he'd undo her pants and make her cum.

JENNIFER: With his mouth he'd make her cum
while she was watching television.

PAM: He'd look beautiful in the light of the television
with his broad shoulders and sandy-coloured hair.

SOPHIE: With his throbbing penis, his juicy boner,
he'd look gorgeous in the light,
and she'd fuck him like that in the TV-blue light;
she'd fuck him and get some release
but instead he's standing there looking.
Just staring at her like she should know what to say.
What the fuck does he want her to say.

BEAUTIFUL MAN: Happy anniversary.

SOPHIE: Fuck.
Fuck fuck fuck fuck fuck.

JENNIFER: That's what she thinks.

SOPHIE: Fuck fuck.

JENNIFER: I'm an ass.

SOPHIE: That's what she thinks.

JENNIFER: I'm an ass.

PAM: And he's looking disappointed.
He's looking like he's been let down.

SOPHIE: That's when she sees it behind him.

JENNIFER: Behind him she can see it.

SOPHIE: The puttanesca in his grandmother's bowl,
the garlic bread in the Tuscan basket,
the salad on the sideboard
and the wine in the decanter.

JENNIFER: The candles burned down to the wick.
What time is it anyway?

SOPHIE: She sees the night she could have had,

JENNIFER: she should have had,

PAM: she would have had if she were somebody else.

SOPHIE: Maybe she could be somebody else.
Get a nine-to-five,
mow the lawn on weekends,
take a photography class.

PAM: He wants to start a family.

JENNIFER: Right, he wants to start a family,
I remember that part.

SOPHIE: She's been putting him off,
convinced him to wait a year,
she'll be promoted to sergeant,
then she'll have more time to think.

JENNIFER: She won't have more time to think.

SOPHIE: No, she won't have more time to think,
but by telling him she'll have more time to think
she's bought herself time to think.

JENNIFER: There's a smell.

SOPHIE: A smell?

JENNIFER: A smell.
Wafting out of the kitchen.
Something sweet.

SOPHIE: Some sort of cake?

JENNIFER: Some sort of pie?

PAM: He's clearly been cooking all day long
to make this special day special for her,

and to top off the meal,
to top it all off,
he decided to bake something special.

JENNIFER: Is something melting?

SOPHIE: Is something burning?

JENNIFER: Is that the smell of charred skin?

SOPHIE: And then she's thinking about her day.
She's been triggered by the cake—

JENNIFER: Or the pie.

SOPHIE: Or whatever it is, she's been triggered,
and she thinks about the reason she couldn't just come home.

JENNIFER: The reason she had to go to the bar
after the day she's had.

SOPHIE: Another victim found.

JENNIFER: Another victim found.

PAM: Another victim found in another basement.

SOPHIE: Hands tied above his head,
strung up like a piece of meat
with his wrists around a hot water pipe.
There were burn marks on his wrists
and she'd suspected he'd been there for days.
His sandy-coloured hair was sweaty,
pasted to his skin.

JENNIFER: Yes, I remember,
it looked like he'd been sweating.

SOPHIE: Made to sweat.

JENNIFER: Made to sweat and bleed.

SOPHIE: There were little incisions on his forearms,
on the backs of his knees,
on his genitals.

JENNIFER: The incisions looked like holes,
like little finger holes with a long stream of blood
trickling from each one.

SOPHIE: She knows it must have taken a long time.
He'd been down there for five days.

JENNIFER: Maybe more.

SOPHIE: Yes, maybe more,
and there was something about his penis.

JENNIFER: About his penis, yes, that's right.

SOPHIE: It looked swollen.

JENNIFER: Did he have a boner?

SOPHIE: I think that was more from the death than the sex.

JENNIFER: Yes, but he did have a boner.

PAM: To me it looked more like a semi.

SOPHIE: Yes, but the swelling wasn't natural.
It wasn't the look of a healthy penis with a death boner.

JENNIFER: No, you're right, the penis looked really sore.

SOPHIE: Swollen and raw and sore like it had been handled again and again.

PAM: And again and again and again.

SOPHIE: She made sure to examine it carefully.
She lifted it up with her pencil.

JENNIFER: I thought it was already up.

SOPHIE: It was semi-up, semi-down,
so she sort of moved it around.

JENNIFER: Yes, she moved his penis around with her pencil.

SOPHIE: He was naked so that was easy.

PAM: Yes, he was completely naked.

JENNIFER: He'd probably been raped.

SOPHIE: Drugged and raped.

JENNIFER: Made to do things with his penis
no one would ever want to do.

PAM: But the incredible thing about it
was the way he looked in the light.
There was something beautiful about the way he was posed
in the light with his glistening sweaty skin

and his hair pasted to his forehead.
He looked so calm in his sweat.

SOPHIE: So much sweat.

JENNIFER: And did she notice his underwear?

SOPHIE: Rosie didn't miss a thing.

PAM: Rosie never misses a thing.

JENNIFER: His torn and bloodied briefs
discarded in a corner.

SOPHIE: A rat licking at the blood.

JENNIFER: A rat, that's right, a rat she kicked away
before she picked up his briefs with the pencil,
with the same pencil she'd used to move his penis.

SOPHIE: To move his swollen semi around.

JENNIFER: Then she put the briefs in a bag.

SOPHIE: An evidence bag to give to the lab
so they could test it for semen and other secretions,
then she looked back at him with a look of pity and pain.

PAM: He hung there looking beautiful.

JENNIFER: Quiet.

SOPHIE: Still.

PAM: Serene.

SOPHIE: And that beauty made Rosie angry.
It made her roaring angry, so she yelled at the forensic team
for starting to bag the body
and you could see what Rosie was thinking.

JENNIFER: In that moment you could see exactly what Rosie was thinking.

SOPHIE: What a waste of a man.

PAM: Of a beautiful man.

SOPHIE: Of a man with such arresting beauty.

JENNIFER: He could have been a father.

SOPHIE: If he wasn't already.

JENNIFER: He could have been a husband.

SOPHIE: If he wasn't already.

JENNIFER: He could have saved the lives of sick children
in the hospital for sick children where he worked.

SOPHIE: And that's when she thought of her boyfriend.

JENNIFER: What was his name?

SOPHIE: That's when she filled with fear.

JENNIFER: Was it Frank?

SOPHIE: It could have been him in that basement.

JENNIFER: Or Joe?

SOPHIE: In that basement it could have been him.

JENNIFER: Does Jason ring a bell?

SOPHIE: Rosie couldn't breathe.

JENNIFER: Sam?

SOPHIE: She had to get out of that basement.

JENNIFER: Carl?

SOPHIE: She had to come up for air.
She looked at him one last time,
at the beautiful man strung up in the basement.
She got close to the body,
frighteningly close to the body.

JENNIFER: I wouldn't have gotten that close.

SOPHIE: But Rosie got close to the body.
She was right beside his face.
And that's when she said in a whisper,
so soft you could scarcely hear.
In a whisper she said:
"I'll find the one who did this."

JENNIFER: That's not what she said.

SOPHIE: She did, she said, "I'll find the one who did this."

JENNIFER: No no.
I'm sure she said in a whisper,
but still loud enough we could hear,
she said, "I'll kill the bitch."

PAM: No she didn't.
Rosie wouldn't be that crass.
Not to him in his beautiful state,
staring up at the basement ceiling,
sweating and bleeding all over himself.
What she said, I'm sure what she said was:
"Good night, sweet prince.
May hosts of angels sing you to sleep."

SOPHIE: That's it.

JENNIFER: Yes, that's it.

PAM: She's tough but she's also a reader.

SOPHIE: A lover of plays.

JENNIFER: Of Shakespeare.

SOPHIE: Because she knows the key to every psychopath
can be found in the plays of Shakespeare.

JENNIFER: And she has a photographic memory,
so she reads them once and knows the lines.

SOPHIE: And she sleeps with a copy of *Hamlet*
under her pillow at night.
She vows never to let such beauty die again
and as she's walking home through the heat of summer—

JENNIFER: I thought it was snowing.

SOPHIE: Snowing, yes, so the crunch of snow
under her feet—

JENNIFER: And the searing pain of the cold north wind reminds her of what it is to be human.

PAM: What it is to be alive.

SOPHIE: But she just can't bear her own humanity so she stops in for a drink at O'Malley's.

JENNIFER: Just one drink, she tells herself.

SOPHIE: Just one drink with old Colleen O'Malley.

JENNIFER: Colleen's the bartender?

SOPHIE: She owns the place but she also tends the bar because it's a dive and that's the way Colleen likes it.

JENNIFER: She likes it that way
because she knows people like Rosie
need to drink in a place that reflects the way they feel.

PAM: Colleen takes one glance at Rosie
and immediately pours her a vodka tonic.

SOPHIE: I thought Rosie drank gin.

JENNIFER: Colleen pours the whiskey
and reaches for the bowl of wasabi peas.

SOPHIE: For the bowl of popcorn.

PAM: For the bowl of in-shell jumbo roasted peanuts she keeps under the bar especially for Rosie.

SOPHIE: And she lets her sit in silence.

JENNIFER: Yes. For the first two drinks she lets her sit in silence
because Colleen can see Rosie's reviewing the case,
going through every bit of evidence she's gathered so far,
but when Rosie signals for a third,
Colleen shakes her head slowly
with the wisdom of a woman who's been down that road herself.

PAM: "Maybe you should stop."

SOPHIE: And they both know she's talking about the whiskey,
but she's also talking about the job.

JENNIFER: Yes, she's talking about the job
because she's seen Rosie in this place before,
she's seen this look on her face before
when she was deep inside that case with the kid
and this time she wonders if Rosie
will survive if she doesn't let it go,
if she doesn't just let it go.

SOPHIE: And Rosie looks up and into Colleen's eyes
and they both say so much with their eyes.

JENNIFER: They're both so good, just so fucking good.

SOPHIE: So when Rosie says, "I can't," she means
a hundred things all at once.

PAM: And Rosie wants another, she still needs another,
but Colleen won't pour her one, which pisses her off,
so she storms out into the street.

SOPHIE: And now she's sitting on the couch
in a stupor with the glass of whiskey Colleen didn't want her to drink
and her boyfriend—

JENNIFER: What was his name?

SOPHIE: He looks at her and he says it again:

BEAUTIFUL MAN: Happy anniversary.

SOPHIE: But when she looks at him now,
when she sees him in this light,
she only sees the dead man in the cellar.

PAM: Looking beautiful.

JENNIFER: But dead.

SOPHIE: And she wants to fuck the dead man.

JENNIFER: No, she wants to fuck her boyfriend.

PAM: Jed?

JENNIFER: She wants to fuck someone but instead she watches TV.

SOPHIE: Yes, and she doesn't say anything to her boyfriend,
she just turns on the TV.

BEAUTIFUL MAN: Unbelievable!

PAM: So he storms from the room.
He's angry.

JENNIFER: Of course he's angry.

PAM: He's crying in the bedroom.

JENNIFER: Is he crying in the bedroom?

PAM: I think we can hear him crying.

JENNIFER: I don't remember hearing him cry.

PAM: He feels betrayed, he feels used, he feels alone.

JENNIFER: That might be true, but we don't see him in the bedroom.

SOPHIE: No, we just see Rosie on the couch
watching an historical drama.

PAM: Would you call it an historical drama?

JENNIFER: Well, there are historical elements
but the series is based on a fantasy novel.

SOPHIE: On a series of fantasy novels, that's right,
but it's basically set in medieval times.

JENNIFER: Right, things are the way they were.

SOPHIE: Class struggle and infant mortality.

PAM: Swords and horse-drawn carts.

SOPHIE: Famine, disease and war.

JENNIFER: But aside from historical elements,
there are dragons and witches and ogres
for the characters to fight.

SOPHIE: And the characters are honest.

JENNIFER: They are true to the emotional stakes of the scene
even when there are ogres.

SOPHIE: Which is just what Rosie needs.

PAM: A fantasy set in an augmented medieval past
acted with honest intention.

JENNIFER: I love the director,
she's so fucking good.

PAM: Everything she does is so fucking good.

SOPHIE: There's the queen.

JENNIFER: Right. Queen Ruth.

PAM: But the peasants call her Queen Ruthless
even though she's doing the best that she can.

SOPHIE: Yes, the crown weighs heavy on her head.

JENNIFER: She's in charge.

SOPHIE: She's the one who makes all the decisions
and there are so many decisions to be made.
Decisions that impact the well-being
of her entire kingdom.
It's a lot to handle.

JENNIFER: A lot to handle, yes, but she's a benevolent leader.

SOPHIE: Benevolent, yes, but cruel when she has to be.
And sometimes she has to be cruel.
Especially to her husband.

JENNIFER: What's his name?

SOPHIE: I can't remember.

PAM: But he looks beautiful in red
so he's always wearing red,
and he smiles dutifully and says things like:

BEAUTIFUL MAN: What is your will, m'lady?

JENNIFER: And his part gets bigger as it goes along,
as the series goes along he becomes
a more important character.

PAM: Yes, a more essential character.

SOPHIE: But for the first five episodes he's either sitting beside
Queen Ruth—

PAM: Looking beautiful in red—

SOPHIE: While her advisors bring her one problem after the next—

JENNIFER: Or sometimes he's naked in their bedroom.

SOPHIE: Yes, she likes to chain him up.

PAM: He likes it too.
You can tell by the look on his face.

SOPHIE: Yes, he likes it too but it's mainly her decision,
because when she's stressed out
the thing that most relaxes her,
that releases all tension,
is to lie on her bed eating grapes
and drinking wine while the king licks her toes like a dog.

JENNIFER: Does he wear a collar?

SOPHIE: Yes there's some sort of collar
attached to a chain.

PAM: And he's hard for it.

SOPHIE: Yes.

PAM: The whole time he's got a boner.

SOPHIE: And you can really see the boner
because he waxes his pubic hair.

JENNIFER: I'm not sure that part's historically accurate.

PAM: That he waxes his pubic hair?

SOPHIE: But you have to be able to see the boner
so I'm glad there isn't hair.

JENNIFER: I like that they show you the boner.
It makes the whole thing more real.

PAM: And I think it's really his boner.

JENNIFER: The actor's?

PAM: What's his name?

JENNIFER: Sometimes they get a boner double if the actor is too shy.
It's written into his contract.

SOPHIE: Yes, I read an article about a man
who was a boner double.

PAM: But the director.

JENNIFER: I love the director,
she's so fucking good.

PAM: The director, she insisted that the actor use his own boner,
which I really just think is so brave.

SOPHIE: I guess, but he's got a great boner,
so I can't imagine it would have been an issue.

JENNIFER: Unless he had injections?

PAM: Or some sort of operation and he was worried we'd see the scars.

SOPHIE: That's possible, yes, but regardless it's worth it
because it makes the whole thing more real.

JENNIFER: Yes, it makes the whole thing more real.

SOPHIE: And Queen Ruth takes her time to deal with the boner.

JENNIFER: Yes, she makes him wait until she's ready.
Sometimes her advisors are in the room
talking to her about various strategies to quash her sister's revolt
and the king is licking her toes
and she's just ignoring him
until she can't ignore him anymore
and she tells her advisors to leave.

SOPHIE: Or even sometimes she doesn't.

JENNIFER: Yes, she doesn't really care
if her advisors are there or not
and sometimes she likes to have them there
so she can demonstrate her power.

PAM: And she yanks at the chain around the king's neck
and pins him to the floor
and slides down upon him
with pointed urgency.

SOPHIE: And at that moment she's able to put aside
all the cares of her kingdom—

JENNIFER: The dragons, the ogres, the plagues.

SOPHIE: She puts all those cares behind her
while she fucks her beautiful man
into making sounds like:

> BEAUTIFUL MAN: Uh uh uh uh uh uh . . . don't stop don't stop
> don't stop.

SOPHIE: But sometimes she has to stop.

JENNIFER: She finishes first and doesn't have time
to wait around for him.

SOPHIE: She's got things on her mind.

JENNIFER: Important things.

SOPHIE: Life or death things.
And it's fine if he wants to fuck all day,
what does it matter to him,
but she's the queen and there are people depending on her.

PAM: But he's so beautiful
with his sandy-coloured hair.

SOPHIE: It doesn't matter.

PAM: He's in earnest, he's depressed.

SOPHIE: Maybe he is but we don't see it.

PAM: We can imagine it.

SOPHIE: But we don't see it.
We only follow the queen, who has important things on her mind.

JENNIFER: Like her sister.

SOPHIE: Yes, her sister.

JENNIFER: From the jungles of the south.

SOPHIE: Her Amazon sister, Di,
who's lusting after the throne.

JENNIFER: She has an army of left-breasted women
who are gaining power in the south.
To prove allegiance to Di,
they sever their right breasts
and sacrifice them to her namesake Diana,
goddess of the hunt;
goddess of her army of left-breasted women,
and they're good at riding horses.

PAM: And they keep their men in cages.

SOPHIE: And the scenes with the sister are terrifying.
She's savage and brutal and wild;
the image of the queen in reverse,
as though one woman had been split in two at birth.

PAM: And there's all this imagery,
I love it when there's imagery:

dark and light,
lions and sheep,
skulls and rainbows.
And the imagery is important
because it makes you think about good versus evil,
nature versus nurture.

JENNIFER: One sister coddled and groomed for the thrown—

PAM: The other never treated with respect.
Never loved as a child.
No one ever let her talk, so she started talking to the animals,
to the horses and field mice and birds of prey,
and one day she flew into a rage
and ran into the woods
and built an ice castle with her hidden power.

JENNIFER: But it was hot in the jungle.

SOPHIE: Yes, it was hot in the jungle,
so she built a palace in the trees
and she prayed to the goddess Diana,
and that's when she changed her name to Di.

JENNIFER: Yes, the gods are characters too, that's right.

SOPHIE: But we only see their feet.

JENNIFER: And their thunderstorms.

SOPHIE: Yes, we see their thunderstorms
when they're really pissed.

JENNIFER: And the gods are always really pissed,
but that doesn't bother Di.
In fact, it fuels her rage.

SOPHIE: Di leads her army into villages.
They attack from the trees with bows and arrows,
they burn the huts and take the food
and make the women decide
whether or not they'll join her army.
If they do, they have to cut off a breast
and throw it in the fire.
If they don't, their heads are put on spikes.

JENNIFER: She's fierce—I like that about her—
and somewhere smouldering under the fire in her eyes,
somewhere deep inside,
is the potential for love.

SOPHIE: So she's just sacked this village
and the ugly men have been slaughtered.
They're bleeding in the dirt
and Di orders the beautiful ones
to stand up straight in a line
because she has this ritual.

JENNIFER: This process of selection.

SOPHIE: This way of deciding which men she wants to keep.

JENNIFER: Which ones she wants for her harem.

SOPHIE: Because she needs the sperm.

JENNIFER: They all need the sperm.

SOPHIE: To make more Amazon warriors.

PAM: But she only wants men who are beautiful.
Ones with the strength to survive.

Preferably ones who can make girl babies,
and if they make too many boy babies they die.

SOPHIE: So she lines them all up before her.

JENNIFER: From tallest to shortest,
and they're naked, of course,
because she's got to examine them thoroughly.
She's got to see which she prefers.

PAM: And their hair is messy
and they haven't shaved
and they're dirty and sullen and sweaty.

JENNIFER: Yes, they're totally covered in sweat.

SOPHIE: And one of them is standing with an arrow through his
shoulder.
He has an arrow protruding through his right shoulder
but still he's standing upright.

JENNIFER: And they have to tear off his shirt around the arrow
and he's in brutal pain, but still he's standing upright.

SOPHIE: And they're all standing there naked.

JENNIFER: Which is historically accurate by the way.
I read it somewhere, this is true.

PAM: But they don't have pubic hair either.

SOPHIE: No, they don't have pubic hair,
which may or may not be historically true,
but aside from the pubic hair it's all honestly true
and they're lined up naked and bleeding,

and if they try to cover their genitals,
if they try to be modest, Di shoots a glance to the Crusher.

JENNIFER: Oh God, I love the Crusher,
she's so fucking good.
The Crusher, yes, and with one glance
the Crusher lumbers over
to where the modest man is standing.

PAM: The beautiful modest man who's trying to cover his genitals
out of politeness, out of nervousness, out of—

JENNIFER: The Crusher takes both of his wrists in one of her enormous hands
and holds them above his head
and with the other hand she takes his balls,
she takes his balls and starts to crush
and she crushes and crushes and crushes his balls
until they're paste inside their sacs,
then she makes another man bite them open
and suck out the paste inside.

PAM: And the beautiful man is screaming terrifying, blood-curdling screams.
He's begging and pleading for death like this:

> BEAUTIFUL MAN: Ahhhhh!!!!
> Ahhhhhh!!!
> Kill me now.
> Kill me, please.
> Ahhhhhh!!!!

JENNIFER: But the Crusher doesn't stop.
And she doesn't kill him quick.
And she makes the ball-sucking man suck the ball paste slower.
She makes him take his time

and she says if he doesn't take his time
he'll have *his* balls crushed next,
so he's on his knees slowly sucking
the ball paste out of the screaming man.

      BEAUTIFUL MAN makes the sound of sucking ball paste out of a ball sac.

And she makes him swallow it down.
Swallow it deep to his soul.
And the other men in line try not to look.
They try not to look at the Crusher crushing balls
or at the man on his knees sucking crushed-up balls,
but their own balls can't help but retreat in empathy
and the director shows a close-up of that.

SOPHIE: I didn't know balls could do that.
Just shrivel back in fear.

JENNIFER: You know it's based on science.
On the empathy of balls.

SOPHIE: Yes, I think I can remember
reading that somewhere.

JENNIFER: It's sort of like telepathy,
like the balls are all connected.

SOPHIE: Which is why they show the close-up of the balls.

PAM: They're beautiful balls.
Terrified balls.
I feel badly for the balls hanging there in a row,
shrivelling back in fear,
trying to crawl up and hide
from the wrath of the mighty Crusher.

JENNIFER: But they know they can't cover them up.
They can't put their hands in front of their genitals,
so they just stand there open for inspection
as Di walks down the line.

PAM: Yes, Di inspects each man,
each new beautiful acquisition, and we know she's on the hunt.
On the hunt for breeders for her army,
and maybe one for herself
because she knows a woman is more fierce
with a baby in the belly,
and she's about to attack Queen Ruthless
so she wants to plant the seed
so she'll be as merciless as possible,
so with the dirt of battle still caked in her hair
she inspects each one by one.
She comes to a stop in front of a man
with a broad chest and sandy-coloured hair.
He can't be much more than eighteen and he's beautiful,
covered in sweat.

SOPHIE: She casually fondles his penis
and he starts to get a boner.

JENNIFER: It's a semi, I think.

SOPHIE: Yes, a semi, but she's learned what she wanted to learn.

JENNIFER: He has an undiscerning penis.

SOPHIE: So she tells him to form a new line.

PAM: She selects another man with small nipples
and sandy-coloured hair.
She pinches a nipple and laughs.
She says, "We'll have to work on these."

SOPHIE: That's right, because the scientist in the clan
has concocted a serum
that makes men start to lactate.

JENNIFER: And just at that moment we see a nanny-man
in the background with a baby on his breast.

PAM: It's beautiful because it's so natural.

SOPHIE: Finally she comes to the one with the arrow through his
shoulder.
His arms are heavy with muscle and exhaustion
from fighting a futile battle.

PAM: He's beautiful.
The most beautiful.
Not sandy-colour-haired like the others.
He has dark skin and dark eyes.

JENNIFER: And this is the first man we see with dark skin,
so he really stands out.

SOPHIE: Yes, he really stands out with his dark skin,
which is why the director cast it this way.

PAM: And back then dark skin was unique.
There weren't as many people with dark skin back then.

JENNIFER: There were lots of people with dark skin back then
but they stayed in countries where other people
also had dark skin.

SOPHIE: Or they were slaves.

JENNIFER: Yes, some people with dark skin were abducted from countries
where other people also had dark skin

and brought to countries where people had light skin
and then they were forced to be slaves.

PAM: Slavery was horrible.

SOPHIE: Yes, slavery was horrible, but this isn't a show about slavery.

JENNIFER: No, you'd need a whole series for that.

SOPHIE: Yes, you'd need a whole series for that,
and you can tell by the casting of this part
that the director might be interested one day in making a series
like that,
but in the setting of this series people stayed where they were,
which is why this director decided to cast light-skinned actors
for all the other parts.

PAM: Because that was historically true for this fictional country.

SOPHIE: And it makes this man stand out
so you wonder where he's really from.

PAM: The character, not the actor.

SOPHIE: Yes, the character, not the actor, but he doesn't speak
so you can't hear an accent,
so we don't get any indication of where he might be from.

JENNIFER: But she gives you a clue with his penis.

PAM: With his penis, yes, the director gives you a clue.

SOPHIE: There's a close-up of his penis
so we can see that he's been circumcised
which means he's probably Muslim.

JENNIFER: Or Jewish, he could be Jewish.

PAM: Do you think the actor they chose
had to get circumcised for the part?

SOPHIE: That was probably in the casting call.

JENNIFER: Yes, the director probably made that clear
when she was looking for an actor to play this part,
that she wanted a man with a circumcised penis.

SOPHIE: Or maybe it was a happy accident.
The director went in for the close-up
and there was the circumcised penis.

PAM: The circumcised penis dripping with sweat.

JENNIFER: I thought that was pee.

SOPHIE: No, it's sweat.
He's sweaty with anticipation,
and even when flaccid his penis is huge,
which is one thing Di likes about him.

JENNIFER: She likes it and so does the cop who's watching the
show on TV
while gulping back another whiskey.

PAM: They all like that he's beautiful, but he's also a good actor,
you can tell, because he says so much with his eyes.
He doesn't have any lines so he has to say it with his eyes.
His dark and beautiful eyes.

SOPHIE: Does this one have a name?

JENNIFER: Probably, but I don't think they say.

PAM: From his eyes you can tell he wants so many things.

JENNIFER: He hates her for destroying his village.

SOPHIE: And for decapitating his fiancée.

JENNIFER: Right, her head is on a spike.

PAM: But at the same time, he can't help but be attracted to Di.
He doesn't want to want her but he simply can't help himself.

SOPHIE: Di examines the arrow that's sticking through his shoulder.

JENNIFER: She bites off the arrowhead with her teeth
and spits it on the ground.

PAM: The beautiful man doesn't make a sound
but he's suffering immensely
as she pulls the shaft of the arrow free.

JENNIFER: Again, he doesn't speak.

SOPHIE: But he breathes.

JENNIFER: Yes, you can hear him breathing.

> *We hear the BEAUTIFUL MAN breathing.*

He breathes as she licks the wound.

SOPHIE: Yes, she licks the wound.
There's a close-up of her sticking her tongue into his wound.

JENNIFER: She's fucking his wound with her tongue.

PAM: And he's in pain.

JENNIFER: It's clear he's in pain.

PAM: But it's also a kind of ecstasy.
You can tell he wants her to do it.
He can't help but feel aroused.

JENNIFER: You can see it on his face
and the director has obviously told him to feel the pain
but also the pleasure.

SOPHIE: Yes, the director, she's told him to feel the pain and the pleasure,
so he does feel the pain and the pleasure
as Di fucks his wound with her tongue,
and in his eye is a single tear.

PAM: A beautiful tear.
A suspended tear.
It lingers in his eye for a moment
before it trickles down his face,
and you can tell he's looking at something.

SOPHIE: Yes, he's looking up at something,
yes, there's something in the distance.

PAM: What is it that he sees?

JENNIFER: It's his fiancée's head on a spike.

PAM: That's it.

JENNIFER: He's looking at his fiancée's head
as he's being tongue-raped
in the hole in his shoulder.

SOPHIE: And we see her face.

JENNIFER: The fiancée's face, you're right, we see it.

PAM: Her ashen face with her dead eyes looking down,
as if she's staring at another woman
tongue-raping her fiancé's wound.
As if she's cursing him from beyond the grave
for letting Di tongue-rape his wound,
which puts the beautiful man in a terrible position,
because in that situation he has no other choice
but to allow his wound to be tongue-raped.
It's either a tongue-rape to the wound
or crush-pasted balls and certain death.
At least this way he can plot his revenge.
At least this way he can avenge his dead fiancée,
if he can only find the means at some point in the future,
if he can only—

JENNIFER: But we don't think about that.
We're thinking about Di because it's at this point we realize we know.

SOPHIE: We know, yes, we realize we know at this moment
that Di has chosen him to be her mate,
so the next shot we see is at night,
that very same night in the harem tent where the new men
are chained up with the old men—

JENNIFER: Not *old* men, of course—there aren't any old men.

SOPHIE: Of course not, no, I just meant the men who had been there
before.

JENNIFER: Yes, I know.
Just thought I'd clarify.

SOPHIE: I hate seeing old men in shows or movies.
It makes me think about death.

JENNIFER: It makes me think about shrivelling.

PAM: It makes me think about killing myself
before I change the channel.

SOPHIE: So the fresh young slaves are licking each other's pricks
to turn on the Amazon warriors
who are trying to get themselves knocked up,
and we see a bunch of them fucking.

PAM: Looking powerful in the light,
in the glow of the firelight,
their single breasts bobbing up and down.

SOPHIE: And we see Di fucking this new slave.

JENNIFER: Do we know his name?

SOPHIE: Not yet but I think we will.
I think he becomes important.

PAM: Important to the plot.

SOPHIE: And important for her character.
For Di's character.
He reveals a lot about her character.
Puts obstacles in her way.
Makes it difficult for her to obtain her goals
in the plot as the story develops.
You just have to wait a few episodes.

JENNIFER: The director wants us to wait a few episodes
to get to know the importance of the male characters.

SOPHIE: The director, I hear, I hear she did a lot of research.

JENNIFER: Yes, a lot of historical research.

SOPHIE: And scientific too.

PAM: She also talked to a psychologist who's an expert
in these types of things.

JENNIFER: They're making a documentary about all the research
she did.

SOPHIE: And she travelled too.
She had interns all over.

PAM: Oh, I heard about the interns.

JENNIFER: Why didn't they speak out sooner,
that's my only question.

PAM: So many beautiful young men.

JENNIFER: They'd just wake up sore?

SOPHIE: And confused, is that it?

JENNIFER: She did it in hotel rooms?

PAM: Sometimes at her home, and these young men,
these beautiful young men, would find bruises in the morning.

JENNIFER: Did she drug them?

SOPHIE: She must have drugged them.

PAM: So many bruises on so much beautiful skin.

SOPHIE: And little incisions, is that right?

JENNIFER: Perfect for a finger.

SOPHIE: Or a tongue.

JENNIFER: Right, a tongue.

PAM: And their penises were swollen.

SOPHIE: I saw a picture of one.

JENNIFER: Shaved and swollen,
it was awful,
but why did he take a picture,
that's my only question.

SOPHIE: I think he wanted a record
of what he thought had happened.

JENNIFER: But why did he decide to post it,
that's my only question.

PAM: Before that they looked so happy.
Have you seen the pictures from before
when they're standing with her posing,
when they're posing in front of a hut
in the Congo or wherever,
on one of her research trips,
and they look so happy together,
so you can understand why they wouldn't have suspected
anything bad would happen,
why they trusted her implicitly
in that circumstance,
in that time of their lives,
in that moment with someone they looked up to,
someone who's important, more important than them in the world,
you can understand what would have compelled them to go

back to her hotel room to discuss the day's adventures,
the day's research, the day's evidence
that what they were doing was important
and necessary and something like reporting
from a war zone but in a fictional context,
you can really understand,
but then the pictures after it happened,
the look of shame in their eyes,
that's what makes me disgusted,
the look of shame in their eyes.

SOPHIE: They could have been husbands.

JENNIFER: If they weren't already.

SOPHIE: They could have been fathers.

JENNIFER: If they weren't already.

PAM: But now they're traumatized.
It will take them years to heal.

SOPHIE: If they ever do, which is why I'm glad they're speaking out,
that they're finally speaking out,
finally finding the courage.

PAM: It's an incredible thing.

SOPHIE: A remarkable thing.

PAM: A beautiful thing.

JENNIFER: I'm not defending her,
not defending the director at all,
but if you're writing and directing a drama like this
with so much violence and historical precedence

and you immerse yourself in the details
of that violence and historical precedence the way an actor would—

SOPHIE: An actor who does the Method.

JENNIFER: —the Method but for directors,
well, you can see how it could seep in.

PAM: I don't know. Did you look at the pictures?

JENNIFER: Sure, of course I looked at the pictures,
and there isn't any excuse for what allegedly happened,
but what I'm talking about is power.

SOPHIE: Power, yes, power is hard.

JENNIFER: Power is extremely hard.

SOPHIE: Which is why Queen Ruth can't be completely transparent
with her subjects as she waits for her Amazon sister to attack.

JENNIFER: Which is why the queen always seems so anxious.

SOPHIE: Which is why the queen always seems so stressed.

JENNIFER: Which is why the queen asks her husband
to organize some sort of distraction.

PAM: But the king isn't sure what she's asking him to do,
so he just stares at her vapidly.

BEAUTIFUL MAN: Ummmm.

SOPHIE: But one of the queen's advisors understands
and orders the players to play a play about a politician.
A politician in ancient Rome.

JENNIFER: A politician named Antonia,
who's the leader of the senate,
and her army have just marched victorious
on another city state.

SOPHIE: Yes, and they're parading through the streets
and the plebs are throwing flowers,
and they want to crown her empress
but Antonia resists.

JENNIFER: She refuses to be crowned
because she believes in the principles
that have been established for organizing
her government, which is what makes her a populist leader.

PAM: Oh yes, the people love her.

SOPHIE: She's popular with the people
because she believes in peoples' rights.

PAM: Like democracy today?

JENNIFER: Something like democracy today,
but not for people who are poor.
And not for men, of course.
Back then men were considered property.
Back then, they couldn't vote.

PAM: I remember learning that.

JENNIFER: Now there's another politician named Cassia
who thinks Antonia's liberal ideals have gotten way out of control.

PAM: And Cassia's very clever—

SOPHIE: Clever but less appealing than Antonia
to the general population.

PAM: She's got a limp, I think.

JENNIFER: That's it, she's got a limp,
she's had some serious trauma.

SOPHIE: Her mother dropped her from a window.

PAM: Her father threw her in a fire.

JENNIFER: She was bitten by a snake
that was hiding in her cradle.

SOPHIE: It was a snake, yes, a snake that bit her leg,
and that leg never reached its full potential.
She tells us it stunted her growth.

JENNIFER: Who tells us it stunted her growth?

SOPHIE: Cassia speaks to the audience.

JENNIFER: Oh yah! I love it when she talks to us,
and the first time she talks to us
it comes as a surprise because we don't know
the players are going to use that theatrical convention.

PAM: Cassia's monologues are so good.

JENNIFER: They're so fucking good.

SOPHIE: Yes, because she's contemplating
all the big questions that plague the human race.

PAM: Like why are we here?
And what about death?
And the nature of good and evil.

JENNIFER: And we get a glimpse into her mind
so you can really understand Cassia as a person,
and that makes the queen who's watching the play
think about that time with her mother at the brook
when she talked about the circle of life
and we get a flashback of that.

SOPHIE: And that makes the cop who's watching the queen
who's watching the politician in the play
think about her own childhood in the inner city,
running around the concrete jungle
with a pack of neighbourhood kids,
laughing at drug dealers and prostitutes,
and she had felt completely invincible,
like nothing bad could ever happen.

JENNIFER: Until the day her brother got shot.

PAM: And they shot him right before her eyes.

JENNIFER: Yes. And there's a flashback of that.

PAM: Of the cop?

JENNIFER: Of the cop, yes, as a child,
cradling her brother's head
with his blood spilling all over her jeans.

SOPHIE: And that's the day she decided to become a cop.

JENNIFER: That's right.

SOPHIE: And as the cop watches the queen watching the play,
we learn that Cassia wants to assassinate Antonia.

PAM: Does she want to assassinate Antonia?

SOPHIE: All the politicians want to assassinate Antonia.

JENNIFER: But Cassia thinks it would be better to shame Antonia publicly,
which is more or less the same as a public assassination,
but she needs information to leverage the shaming,
which is why Cassia starts sleeping with Antonia's husband.

PAM: He's beautiful, really quite stunning.
He's played by an actor much younger
than the actor who plays Antonia
and he's just so beautiful
with his sandy-coloured hair.

JENNIFER: And we see his penis throughout.
And occasionally we see his boner.

SOPHIE: We get flashes of his penis
and occasionally his boner because he only wears a tunic,
which is historically true.

PAM: He has a very beautiful penis
and an even more beautiful boner
and he doesn't say a thing.
When he's in a scene he's quiet.
In fact, he may have lost his voice.

JENNIFER: In fact, I think his tongue was cut out
by an evil dictator when he was just a boy.

PAM: He has a beautiful ass as well.

JENNIFER: You're right.
I'm distracted by the boner,
but he does have a great ass too.
And when Cassia has him where she wants him,
when his penis is a boner,
she gets him to start leaking information.

PAM: He can't tell her, exactly,
because he doesn't have a tongue,
and he can't write it on wax tablets
because he never learned to read,
but what he *can* do,
what he is very good at,
is scribbling symbols in the dirt.

JENNIFER: Yes, he scribbles symbols in the dirt
on the floor of the Colosseum.

PAM: "And we don't know what his name is, do we?"

SOPHIE: That's what the queen whispers to her husband
as she's watching Antonia's husband fuck Cassia in the play.

PAM: "Do we know the husband's name?"

JENNIFER: It gets a bit confusing
because Antonia has more than one husband.

SOPHIE: Of course, that was allowed.

JENNIFER: But they all look the same because they are triplets,
which is why the parts are all played
by the same actor in the play in the show in the movie.

PAM: "Have all their tongues been removed?"

JENNIFER: That's what the queen asks her husband.

PAM: The advisor who's instructed the players to play says,
"Yes, it was a policy back then to remove the tongues of boys."

SOPHIE: So Antonia has three husbands,
and because Cassia isn't sure which is which
she has to sleep with them all.

JENNIFER: And the queen's still confused about which one is which
but the advisor says it doesn't really matter.

PAM: Because they're all so beautiful, really,
and that's what's important for the plot,
for the other characters making choices
to propel the action of the play.

SOPHIE: But the cop doesn't care about the queen's confusion,
she just wants to know what happens in the play.

JENNIFER: Well, Cassia has learned from one of the husbands
that Antonia is planning to make an important announcement
to a crowd in the public square
and Cassia thinks this is the perfect moment
to carry out her plan.

PAM: Doesn't it have to do with men?

JENNIFER: Doesn't what have to do with men?

PAM: The announcement.

SOPHIE: Yes. Antonia has a thing about men.

JENNIFER: Right. She has a thing about trying to get men
to speak for themselves.

PAM: Which is really a challenge without any tongues.

JENNIFER: Antonia has a very thorough understanding
of her own privilege.

SOPHIE: Yes, she's very aware of her privilege,
which is why she starts every speech like this:

PAM: "As a dark-skinned female, I enjoy privileges
many can only dream of.
And I take my privilege very seriously."

JENNIFER: I like that she takes it seriously.
So many women don't acknowledge the fact
that their privilege has given them an advantage.

SOPHIE: And the fact that she states it so clearly.

PAM: Yes.

SOPHIE: The fact that she acknowledges it so blatantly.

PAM: Yes.

SOPHIE: It makes you respect her more.

PAM: Yes.

JENNIFER: It makes you want her to be your leader.

SOPHIE: Because she's aware.

PAM: Yes.

SOPHIE: And Antonia uses her privilege for good instead of evil.

JENNIFER: Which is exactly what the queen is doing.

SOPHIE: Which is exactly what the cop is doing.

JENNIFER: They aren't the ones who have been abusing their power.

SOPHIE: They aren't the ones who have been acting inappropriately.

PAM: And it's a relief for them all to finally see a story
that makes them feel good about their powerful positions.

JENNIFER: Antonia's signalling to someone.

PAM: To one of her slaves.

JENNIFER: To one of her husbands.

SOPHIE: To one of her children, yes.
She is inviting one of her sons
to join her on the stage.

PAM: A hush falls over the crowd because it is very rare
for a boy to have the privilege of joining his mother on the stage.

SOPHIE: It is an incredibly risky move that would have seen any other leader
instantly deposed, which is why Cassia is smiling.

JENNIFER: Yes, Cassia is smiling
because this is the moment she's been waiting for.

PAM: Antonia's son is standing on the stage.

JENNIFER: He must be about ten.

SOPHIE: He's eight.

PAM: He's only five years old.
He looks back at his mother
and she gives him a smile and a nod.

JENNIFER: He takes a deep breath,
he opens his mouth,
and then he starts to sing.

BEAUTIFUL MAN: *(singing)* Every rock and stream and tree—

SOPHIE: And no one can believe it.

JENNIFER: His tongue is still intact.

SOPHIE: Antonia has not removed the tongue of her son.

JENNIFER: He's singing their national anthem.

SOPHIE: He's singing an original ballad.

PAM: He's singing a pastoral folk song that reminds them of the past,
of the days before tongues were removed,
and boys, beautiful boys like Antonia's beautiful boy,
were free to sing pastoral folk songs in the countryside
while tending the animals and completing household chores.

SOPHIE: And it's instantly clear to everyone watching
that cutting out the tongues of boys
was one step too far.

PAM: Boys should be celebrated.

JENNIFER: Men too.

PAM: That's right.
Boys and men should be celebrated.

Worshiped even.
Placed on the highest pedestals
as a reminder of wholesome purity.

SOPHIE: And that's when they all start to sing.

JENNIFER: It's incredible.

PAM: The crowd all starts to sing along
to the familiar pastoral folk song.

JENNIFER: The men can't articulate the words, of course,
because their tongues have been removed,
so it sounds a bit more like this:

> *The BEAUTIFUL MAN sings without a tongue.*

SOPHIE: But that doesn't matter.

PAM: Not a bit.

SOPHIE: Because all of them are connected.
All the men agree that Antonia
has understood their plight.
She will give them a voice.

JENNIFER: Or speak *for* them, rather,
so the future looks sunny and bright.

SOPHIE: Except for Cassia.

JENNIFER: Yes, except for Cassia.

SOPHIE: Cassia slinks down a back alley
and makes her way to her favourite hole in the wall,
a dingy little taverna where the wine is overflowing

and she can let herself be distracted
by one of their infamous puppet plays.

PAM: It's a comedy.

SOPHIE: The queen breathes a sigh of relief.

JENNIFER: So does the cop who's watching the queen
who's watching the politician sit in front of the puppet stage.

SOPHIE: Out pops a puppet woman.
She has an intricately carved face
with eyes that move, eyelids that blink
and a jaw on a string so when the puppet speaks
her jaw moves up and down.
She's a cavewoman and her costume has been draped appropriately
to signal that she's a cavewoman.

JENNIFER: She wears a leopard-print dress
and she has strong and capable hands that can curl into a fist
when the puppeteer decides the cavewoman needs
to curl her fingers into a fist.

SOPHIE: We're told her name is Urrr and when she does things like
sit on a rock that resembles an armchair, she says:

PAM: "Urrrrr."

JENNIFER: Which is funny.

SOPHIE: So Urrr stands up and sits down again.

PAM: "Urrrrr."

JENNIFER: The politician is relieved to discover
that she has seen this particular puppet play before.

SOPHIE: At least two or three times.

PAM: At least five or six times,
which is great because the last thing
the politician needs right now is to follow a new storyline.

JENNIFER: To have to figure out the details.

PAM: To have to really pay attention.

JENNIFER: What the politician really needs now
is to dull her senses with a light, familiar puppet play.

SOPHIE: Urrr starts to complain about the day she's had
wrestling woolly mammoths and saber-toothed tigers.
In fact, she's just dragged a dead wildebeest back from the wild,
which lies bleeding by the fire waiting to be skinned.
Urrr just wants to relax.
She wants a drink.
She says—

PAM: "Urrrr!"

JENNIFER: That's when the husband,
I guess it's the husband but he looks rather young—

SOPHIE: It's the husband, I'm sure, but at first he looks like some sort
of ape,
like he's just crawled out of the forest.

JENNIFER: An ape, that's right, he resembles an ape
because he's walking on all fours.

PAM: He enters on all fours, but when he gets into the cave
he comes to a stand,
and when he stands upright we can see that he's beautiful.

He's got a beautiful smile and sandy-coloured hair
and he smiles at his wife, Urrr.

SOPHIE: Yes, but he only smiles because that's all he *can* do.

JENNIFER: Right, that's all he *can* do because his face is carved
out of wood, so the expression on his face is fixed.

PAM: But it's a beautiful expression
and you can tell from his expression that he just adores his wife.

JENNIFER: He adores her, yes, but she also drives him nuts.

SOPHIE: Yes, she also drives him nuts because she's always up to antics.

JENNIFER: Up to antics, yes.
She's always trying to fix things with her best friend Grrr,
but everything gets broken instead of getting fixed
and the husband's the one who has to clean up the mess,
so he starts to sigh a lot.

SOPHIE: That's right, he sighs.

BEAUTIFUL MAN sighs.

JENNIFER: And it's funny.

SOPHIE: Yes, it's funny when he sighs but even funnier when Urrr
is doing
all the crazy things she does, and this evening,
this particular evening, Urrr's asleep in her armchair rock
and the husband comes in.
He sees the carcass of the wildebeest
lying in the living room right beside the fire.

BEAUTIFUL MAN sighs.

He sees the mud dragged all across the floor.

BEAUTIFUL MAN sighs.

He sees the lice crawling out of Urrr's hair.

BEAUTIFUL MAN sighs.

PAM: He looks at Urrr asleep
and drooling and snoring and scratching herself.

BEAUTIFUL MAN sighs.

SOPHIE: The politician has started to laugh.

JENNIFER: The puppet husband tries to clean the mud out from under
Urrr's feet
but she kicks him in the balls.
He tries to kill the lice as they jump into the air
but Urrr rolls over and punches him in the face.
He tries to pull a fur blanket over her
but she grabs him around the throat and starts to throttle him.

SOPHIE: Yes, she starts to throttle him, but she doesn't think it's him
and that's what's incredibly funny.
Urrr is dreaming so she thinks it's a wildebeest
and she starts to strangle him with all her might
and his wooden face doesn't change,
which makes it even more funny.

JENNIFER: The politician is laughing out loud.
She's laughing so hard tears fall from her eyes.
Tears are falling from her eyes with laughter,
and when Urrr finally comes to her senses,
when she realizes exactly what she's doing,
she throws her husband across the cave and he lands on the

carcass of the wildebeest, which explodes blood
all over the husband puppet,
all over the curtains of the puppet theatre,
all over the politician who's sitting in the front row,
and the queen is laughing now,
and the cop has just started to smirk.

SOPHIE: Urrr makes elaborate excuses as Urrr tends to do.
She's a good wife, a kind wife,
but she's always getting into trouble.
Leaves the kids in a tree for hours,
tries to build a "Woman Cave" out of pine branches,
which collapses in on itself.
She's always doing silly things like forgetting anniversaries,
and on this occasion,
on this particular occasion, she's just throttled her husband
and how can you apologize for that.
What can you possibly say except:

PAM: "Urrrrr."

JENNIFER: The politician looks like she might pee her pants
and the queen is laughing out loud.
Even the cop has her hand over her mouth
trying not to spray a mouthful of whiskey
all over the coffee table.

SOPHIE: Urrr apologizes profusely and her husband sighs again.

JENNIFER: That's when Urrr gets horny.

SOPHIE: Right, she always gets horny
when she sees blood splatter.
But most of the time
when she sees blood splatter
she's out in the middle of the wild

and her hands are covered in blood
and there's predators lurking
so she's got to drag back the beast.

JENNIFER: But here, in her cave, sitting there looking at her husband
in the aftermath of strangulation,
his face splattered with the blood of the beast,
a welt pushing up under his eye,
well, she sees an opportunity.

PAM: And he's beautiful.
He's always beautiful, Urrr thinks,
but here in the light of the fire,
catching his breath and splattered in blood,
there's really something special.

JENNIFER: It's then that she notices her husband
is wearing a new loincloth.

SOPHIE: Right. She hasn't seen that loincloth before
and it's cut in a particular way
that gives her reason to suspect it wasn't cheap.

PAM: "So you're spending all my money on stupid shit like that?"

SOPHIE: Yes, that's exactly what she says.

PAM: "Spending all my money to look like a whore?"

SOPHIE: And his puppet head tilts down, although he doesn't say a thing.

PAM: His expression remains the same, but you get the sense he's
disappointed.

SOPHIE: Disappointed or embarrassed?

JENNIFER: It's a little difficult to tell.

PAM: "Take it off."

SOPHIE: His body gets still.

PAM: "Take it off, I said."

SOPHIE: The husband caveman shakes his head,
yes—slowly he shakes his head—
he just wants to go to bed,
at least that's what I think we're meant to think
but it's really difficult to tell.

PAM: "Take it off."

SOPHIE: She says it again.

PAM: "Don't make me have to get up
and come over there to do it myself."

JENNIFER: And we all suspect she's setting us up
for some sort of laugh.
We all have a sense that that's about to happen
but she's so serious when she says it,
and her puppet eyes in the fire light
have a sort of menacing effect.

SOPHIE: And the politician can't wait any longer
for the puppeteer to decide it's time
to remove the loincloth.
So she reaches into the puppet stage
and pulls the loincloth from the beautiful puppet man
to reveal his enormous
wooden
boner.

JENNIFER: It's gigantic!

PAM: Enormous!

SOPHIE: Colossal!

JENNIFER: It's almost the size of an actual boner
but on a little wooden puppet guy.

SOPHIE: And everyone's in stitches.
Everyone's insane with bellyache laughter
rolling around and crying and biting cushions
to make it stop, make the laughter stop,
make it stop.

PAM: "Come closer."

JENNIFER: That's what Urrr says next, but it's difficult to hear her
because of the roar of the laugh.
So she stokes the fire with a stick
and then she says it again.

PAM: "Come closer."

JENNIFER: And the laughter fades a bit.
We all want to hear what Urrr's going to say.

PAM: "Come closer."

JENNIFER: She says once more and the puppet man
seems to shudder with fear.

SOPHIE: He may have shuddered with fear,
or it may have been anticipation.

JENNIFER: Yes, it may have been in anticipation
of what he knows will happen next,
but he still doesn't come closer, so she says:

PAM: "Come closer or I'll bash you in the fucking head."

SOPHIE: He steps closer.
The fire is between him and his wife.
He steps closer as she whispers:

PAM: "Hit yourself."

SOPHIE: He does.

PAM: "Hit yourself again."

SOPHIE: He hits himself again.

PAM: "Harder."

SOPHIE: He hits himself harder.

PAM: "Harder."

SOPHIE: He does it again.

PAM: "Harder!"

SOPHIE: She says one more time,
and then she hands him the stick
she's been holding in the fire.

PAM: "Burn a hole in your skin."

SOPHIE: He takes the stick but hesitates.

PAM: "Burn a hole in your skin."

SOPHIE: He turns the stick toward his inner thigh.

PAM: "Burn a hole in your skin."

SOPHIE: He does. But he cannot make a sound.

PAM: "God, you're beautiful."

SOPHIE: She says as she starts to touch herself.

PAM: "You're such a beautiful man."

SOPHIE: She proceeds to masturbate.

JENNIFER: And the politician realizes she's got her own hand
tucked into her tunic and she looks at the bartender
to see if she's noticed she's started to touch herself,
but the bartender's fingering herself as she watches beauty suffer,
and watching the bartender masturbate
makes the politician even more horny
so she starts to fuck one of Antonia's husbands
who has just wandered into the taverna,
and then everyone else starts to fuck one another,
and watching this Roman orgy, the queen can't help but lick her lips
as she lifts her skirts and grabs the advisor by the face
and signals for her husband to fuck the advisor from behind
while the advisor is making her cum,
and watching all that fucking
the cop can't help but feel aroused
so she downs her whiskey.

SOPHIE: She turns off the TV.

JENNIFER: She walks down the hall to the bedroom and sees her boyfriend lying on his half of the bed.

SOPHIE: He's lying with his back to the door.

JENNIFER: She likes the shape of his back.

PAM: His beautiful back.

SOPHIE: She can tell he has been crying.

JENNIFER: She takes off her badge.

SOPHIE: She takes off her gun.

JENNIFER: She takes off all her clothes.

SOPHIE: She slips herself in behind him.

PAM: Do we still not know his name?

SOPHIE: She puts her hand into his pyjamas;
she grips his penis
and rubs it to a boner.

JENNIFER: She says she's sorry.

SOPHIE: She says she loves him.

PAM: She kisses the back of his neck.
She smells his skin.
She tastes his sweat.

JENNIFER: She is thinking about the queen thinking about the politician thinking about the cavewoman.

SOPHIE: No she's not.

PAM: She's only thinking about her boyfriend.

SOPHIE: No she's not.

JENNIFER: No she's not.

PAM: No she's not.

SOPHIE: But she doesn't tell him that.

part 2

With pace.

BEAUTIFUL MAN: I wasn't going to start dying my hair, thought I'd let it grey gradually, gracefully, but for me it started early, last year just after I turned thirty, and once it started, it really started and it irritated me: bits of white mixed in with the dark and I've never been the type of woman who wears a lot of makeup—maybe a bit to go out now and then—but not every day, and girls in the bathrooms at high school and university would say, "You're so lucky, you don't need to wear makeup," which I know is a backhanded compliment, the type of thing conventionally pretty girls say to justify the attention they get for being conventionally beautiful, like if they admit they have to work to be beautiful no one will resent them for being beautiful because it is something they work at, but the consequence for being that type of girl is that she relies on the compliments of boys and men around her to exist in the world and even then I could see her trajectory. That girl. I knew her conventional beauty was intrinsically linked to a societal obsession with youth and that her youth would fade in the not-too-distant future, so constructing an identity based on appearance would only lead to a future of heartache and a sense of confusion; a solid fork in the road. A before and after youth. A traumatic moment when that girl realizes that heads are no longer turning and that leads to questions like who am I? and what do I want? and what have I been doing all these years? And some women never come back from that moment.

They rail against age, investing in skin creams and hair dyes and
makeup and surgeries, even, yes, some of those women go on to have
surgeries, especially if their breasts don't recover from breastfeeding—
still when I have kids I'll definitely breastfeed because we all know
breast is best and I'll try to have a natural drug-free childbirthing
experience because c-sections are overprescribed although sometimes
necessary, but either way our bodies carry the push and pull and tear
and scars of childbirth and our bellies sag, our stomach muscles separate, our veins throb to the surface of our legs so if you've tied yourself
to beauty from a very young age, that's it, you're screwed because
there's no going back from childbirth, and what's a woman without a
child. And a partner, of course. And a career. What's a woman without
a child and a partner and a career.

There are parts of my body that I hate. Truly hate. I don't hate anything more than I hate those parts of my body.

Finally I got fed up with looking at the bits of grey in my hair so I
went to the hairdresser and asked her to dye it and got a fantastic
haircut, one of those haircuts you *know* looks really great, and then she
styled it for me but I always hate the stuff she uses to style my hair—
the gels and sprays and creams smell awful and I get very aware that I
don't smell like myself and my hair gets so stiff, but I never want to say
anything because my hairdresser always seems so proud of the way she
styles my hair so I let her style my hair even though I know it costs
me more for her to style it but I don't want her to feel bad because
it really is a great cut so then I go home and have a shower and do
my hair the way I like it and think tonight is one of those nights I'm
going to make an effort so I put on makeup and an outfit I know looks
good on me and go out to meet some friends at a bar to celebrate my
best friend's birthday and as I walk to the subway I feel this energy,
this energy from other people I usually see directed at other women,
energy that makes me laugh to myself and thank God I'm not one of
those women who has to put up with receiving this kind of energy
every day, craving this kind of energy every day, but tonight it's fun;
I feel like a tourist in a foreign country and I'm letting myself enjoy

the ride because I'm confident enough to say what I think and excel at my work so I allow myself to enjoy this feeling of being looked at, this feeling of mild objectification without worrying that I've compromised my integrity, but it's still strange to discover that all the men I interact with are more polite, more attentive, more jokey-jokey, more eager to please, and in spite of myself I am enjoying the attention and the man sitting next to me says I have a beautiful smile. He also says he's positive that the pinot noir we are drinking is the very best of its year. He's wrong. It has a jarring acidity and is one of the most overpriced on the menu. It's mediocre, at best. I imagine telling him he's wrong and can't help myself from projecting his embarrassment into the moment after I tell him. I can't help myself feeling bad for him but the wine isn't good, it really isn't good so I politely disagree and suggest a 2016 Invivo Central Otago Pinot from New Zealand if he wants an exceptional pinot. He looks amused rather than embarrassed and explains, in great detail, the proper way to taste wine. He says I'm probably tasting it wrong, most people do, it's not my fault but he went on a wine tour of the Napa Valley so he knows how to taste wine the proper way. I tell him I was a sommelier at a restaurant before I went to law school, so I do, in fact, know how to taste wine. He's red in the face, but still not deterred, will not concede that I know what I'm talking about, is not prepared to back down, so I'm thinking I'll just leave it at that, I'll just let him think he's won and laugh about it later with my friend whose birthday it is, with my friend who is about to blow out the candles on her cake. While I'm watching her, he leans in close to my ear and whispers, "Show me." That's what he leans in and says. "Show me how you taste wine." And he's got this grin on his face that looks like he's joking but there's a strange sort of menace behind it. A strange sort of dare. Of course, I don't want to show him, but I also don't want to make a big deal. It's my friend's birthday and this guy is just a jerk. He's an asshole, fine, who's friend is he anyway? He's probably someone's boyfriend and she's watching him flirt with me, but if I let him think he's getting to me, I'll be the one who looks stupid; I'll be the one who looks like I'm taking a joke way too seriously and in some sort of way he'll have won. So I pick up my glass, swirl it around, stick my nose and mouth inside, inhale the fumes of the repulsive pinot and then take a sip, swishing it back and forth in my mouth, then I swallow. He observes me carefully and when I finish he says, "Not bad." He then proceeds to give me pointers and demonstrates again. He encourages me to take his advice and try it once more but I can't bear his patronizing tone, so I excuse myself and go to the ladies' room.

I was always a fast swimmer. Gord Hudson and I were the fastest in grade five and at the end of each swim class we would race. Battle of the sexes, so the other girls were always happy when I won. I beat him every time. Every time, though it was close; he was fast but I was faster and I was so strong in the water, reaching out and over and kicking like a menace, holding my breath for as many strokes as possible, and I always won—I always won until the day I didn't. And I knew it wasn't a fluke. He was growing into the body of a man and I would never win again.

I hate when I apologize. It's so disgustingly weak. Especially in an email.

Dear so and so,

Hey, what's up. I hope you're having a wonderful day.

Sorry to spring this on you right before lunch, but I'm just writing to ask if you could send me the thing you said you'd send me yesterday. You probably have a note somewhere from our meeting last week when we decided you were going to send me that thing yesterday? If it's okay with you, I'd love it if you could send it to me in the very near future.

Thanks so much, you're the best.

I look at myself in the bathroom mirror and decide to put on more lipstick. I can't believe I'm refreshing my lipstick because refreshing lipstick is a thing women do in movies and I don't usually wear lipstick so it feels like a bit of a self-betrayal. I always proudly refuse to tie my self-esteem to false images of myself and yet tonight it feels so good, for some reason it feels so good to be refreshing my lipstick in the bathroom mirror of a restaurant right next to a woman who is a woman who regularly refreshes her lipstick. She smiles at me conspiratorially. "Nice colour," she says. "Oh, thanks," I say. I watch myself feel a boost and start to wonder if there is something to this costume, something in this attitude that suits me. What have I missed out on? Could I have been seen more? Been respected more? Would I have gone further in my career? Who am I? and what do I want? and what have I been doing all these years?

When I feel bad I torture myself with past humiliations. Like that time I was taking a new associate around the firm and we get to the law library and there's this woman, this wonderful librarian who keeps everything in order, and she's not the type of person who draws attention to herself, not an extrovert like many of the lawyers, so she just does her job and does her job well and I'm not the type of lawyer who ignores people like her, not the type of person who is blind to the faces of people behind counters; in fact, I pride myself on getting to know peoples' names and remembering those names, even hard to remember names like Jameela Jamil and Saoirse Ronan and Ta-Nehisi Coates, but this woman, this librarian has a name that's easily recognizable for the Western European ear, so without even thinking much about it I said, "And this is Donna. Donna is the most incredible librarian you will meet in your life. All of this, this is Donna." And there was this look on her face, on the librarian's face, this agonized look of confusion and this desire, this desire I could see on her face to crawl under something, to hide, to run, but instead she opened her mouth and said, "It's Deirdre, actually." And I died. I crumbled. I caved in on myself realizing that I had put Deirdre—not Donna—in the most uncomfortable situation and how did I not remember her name. Had I used the wrong mnemonic device when I memorized it in the first place? Or had someone else called her Donna and I'd just picked it up? But now Deirdre clearly thought I was one of those people, those people who don't pay attention to the people behind counters, and Deidre's self-esteem, I saw it shrink, I saw it diminish even though she tried to recover and I tried to make a joke out of it; so when I'm at my worst I remember that moment, that moment I crushed someone with the wrong name. I have a list of small humiliations like that I cycle through when I'm teetering on the edge of hating myself. They pop into my mind in flashes and I cringe to myself—I actually cringe—to think of what an idiot I am, what a fucking idiot.

Shit. I'm bleeding. I forgot I was bleeding. How could I forget I was bleeding, shit. I look through my handbag but the handbag I've brought is the fancy one, the only little black bag I have, and of course there are no tampons inside. Usually I'm throwing tampons all over the place—I go to get my keys and have to wade through a swamp of tampons at the bottom of my bag before I find them but tonight, of course, there's nothing there. I ask the lipstick woman if she has a tampon. "I have a pad?" she says helpfully, and I thank her, of course, and I take it of course, but a pad?! Really? Who wears fucking pads, especially on a night out, but of course I need something so I go in the stall and squat over the toilet and yank on the string of my tampon and it's soaked through so it plops into the toilet looking like a dead mouse and I don't want to sit down because it's a public toilet so I squeeze my bag under my left armpit, wipe myself, unwrap the enormous pad and stick it to my underwear, but the pad is much bigger than my underwear so it sticks to my thighs when I pull them up. I flush the toilet and waddle out of the stall with a feeling of secret shame.

When I return to the table, I look for a seat far away from the jerk with the wine but he's waving me back and I don't see anywhere else to sit. It looks like the guy beside him is also eager for me to return and as I move toward them I try to think of an excuse to leave but when I get to the table the wine guy apologizes, says his friend told him off for mansplaining and he doesn't want to be the type of guy who mansplains and did I really think that's what he was trying to do? If I did think he was mansplaining, he's genuinely sorry, he's just very enthusiastic about wine and his friend tells him off for making a non-apology apology and tells him he should never use the word "if" when making an apology and looks to me for approval. When I don't say anything, the friend says he overheard me saying that I was a sommelier and would I be kind enough to sit down and tell them a bit about wine—he promises neither one of them will interrupt. I don't want to do a lecture on wine, but I can tell they both need me to absolve them of their casual offences and reassure them that I know they aren't the bad guys everyone has been talking about. They are responsive to criticism and are open to self-change and they really aren't bad guys. I can tell they're not bad guys but as I stand there I have a sense of dread that reminds me of my performance review.

Every year I get a fantastic performance review, so I wasn't scared when I went in for my performance review today. Well, I was a little bit nervous, I'm always a little bit nervous, but I'm the top of my group, of my cohort at the firm: "Keep doing what you're doing. You're doing amazing, keep it up," that's what they always say because I'm smarter than everyone else. That's not ego, that's just true and I work fast and I work hard. Really, most people do well in their performance review except Jason. Jason is all talk and no work so Jason always gets a shitty review. And I know Jason always gets a shitty review because he tells everyone. Laughs about it. Doesn't care if everyone knows that they told him to stop coasting, stop bullshitting, stop relying on charm—did I mention he's very charming—good-humoured, good-looking too and he's a fun guy to have at a party so I'd always assumed that's why they didn't fire him, just told him to get down to work because his detail work is sloppy. There are spelling errors, for God's sake, and every year he just seems to scrape by but this year I go in for my review and they tell me I need to start working harder. And I'm like, what? I work my ass off, you know I work my ass off, and they say yes but I need to start focusing on the big picture. If I want to make partner, I need to stop dotting Is and crossing Ts and start bringing in clients. Well, I'm shocked because no one's mentioned this before. No one has said this is what I'm aiming for, this is what I need to focus on, but I guess that makes sense, yes, I guess the way a law firm works is someone brings in clients and they tell me I need to get out there, meet people, schmooze, sit in on some meetings with some of the larger clients and go out drinking afterwards, start talking, stop listening, stop behaving so well, start rocking the boat. Well of course now Jason's in his element. Comes out of his review nearly singing because the rules have changed, suddenly the rules have changed and if there's anything Jason knows how to do it's rock the boat, slap backs, laugh loudly, drink like a fish and I realize he has a summer law school student following him around, taking notes, doing research, crossing his Ts because, let's face it, Jason's not much of a detail guy. He never has been. He never sweats the small stuff and that's what's so great about him, so it's important that he has someone who can do all that busy work while he brings in the clients.

I always thought I did badly on exams even though I always aced them.

It's been a good night, a really good night, and my best friend looks happy. She truly looks happy and that's what I love about her—she lives in the moment and people see that, people love how much fun she is and she's the type of person who's very active on social media; it doesn't seem to get her down so she keeps up with everyone's birthday so she gets so much love on her birthday; everyone wants to celebrate her so that makes me think I should stop being so cynical about the whole social media thing.

As I'm walking home I become aware of the bareness of my legs, of the tightness of my skirt, of the click of my heels on the sidewalk, of the group of men on the corner, of the cliché of this whole situation. Me dressed up like a pretty girl walking home alone in the dark and I probably should have taken an Uber but now I'm only five blocks away, just five blocks away from my apartment, so I just have to walk strong, show no fear because men don't gang rape women anymore. That only happens in cop shows or fantasy shows, maybe I should cross the street. I feel the breath in my chest and the weight of the lipstick on my lips. Don't they say lipstick makes your mouth look like a vagina? I don't want my mouth to look like a vagina. I draw my jacket around me, squeeze my purse under my arm and think about my friend who has short hair and on her way home at night she walks like a man. She purposefully walks like a man. Curls her shoulders forward, takes large strides, takes up space the way men take up space and no one bothers her. Has their behaviour changed? Have they stopped talking? Are they glancing over at me? What the fuck am I doing? I know there is no shame in fear, it's a perfectly normal response to this type of situation and I shouldn't feel ashamed to listen to my body but it feels like it would be embarrassing to cross to the other side of the street. Like I'm conceding that they are more powerful than me, like I know they could do something horrible, might do something horrible, like I think they're the type of men who would do something horrible when really they're just standing on the street corner making plans to study the next day, plans to watch the game together, plans for brunch in the morning and I don't want to make nice men feel like I think they're the type of men that women like me should be afraid of so I just keep walking forward even though some small part of me is screaming to turn around and walk back in the other direction, or pretend to get a call, that's it, and then go back in the other direction, but I don't want to fumble with my phone, it's a new phone, a nice phone, and pulling it out right now might make them think about stealing it when they hadn't even thought about stealing anything at all, what am I thinking? They are just men. Just a group of young men. Just a group of nice young men standing on a corner. But sometimes nice young men standing on a corner do stupid things when they're together, especially when they've been drinking. Have they been drinking? Of course they've been drinking but they don't look menacing, they really do look like good guys, but still, this is an act of trust. And also a kind of dare. A dare to the system that has raised me. To the system that has raised them. I am trusting that their parents have taught them to respect people. That their teachers have taught them about consent and fear and that with the power of their bodies, the size of their bodies, comes great responsibility. Their size is a relatively new realization for them. They have only recently grown into their bodies so their power is also new. It's been building since they were ten years old, since they first won that race in the pool and their feet grew bigger and their voices got deeper and they could stretch out their arms and lift heavy things and when their teachers said things like, "I need two strong boys," they felt their power grow and stopped worrying about dotting Is or crossing Ts. Young men do crazy things when they are together. The adrenaline starts pumping and they feel invincible and they don't think about consequences, which is why they are such excellent weapons of war and the better-looking young men are the worst. They haven't been beaten down by jocks or laughed at by pretty girls who wear lipstick and think of themselves as beautiful and these boys are pretty good looking. They've noticed me now. They've stopped talking and have turned around to look at me as I walk toward them. A couple back up on the grass behind them, a few steps back from the curb, creating a narrow corridor for me to walk through if I don't miscalculate my trajectory, if I don't stumble as I walk through, if they all stay exactly where they are. What the fuck am I doing? I am walking into a circle of lions, a circle of sharks, a circle of men, and they're all watching me approach. Looking at my face at my legs at my shoulders at the vein in my neck that is pounding with fear.

But still I keep on walking.

Still I keep on walking.

> *BEAUTIFUL MAN exits.*
> *Long beat.*
> *The following text is spoken with lots of space.*

s: That was weird.

p: Yah.

Awkward.

s/j: Yah.

j: Why was that so weird?

s: We should have kept talking.

j: It was weird to stop talking.

Like, if she'd been wearing a track suit and walking a dog—

p: / Totally different.

s: Totally fine.

But she can wear whatever she wants.

p: / Of course.

j: I didn't mean . . .

p: My mouth got really dry.

s: We should have crossed to the other side of the street.

p: Shit.

j: Yah, but it felt like it was too late.

s: You're right, that would have been weird.

p: So weird.

j: *She* could have crossed / the street?

s: She shouldn't have to cross the street.

p: Of course not.

s: It's not her responsibility to . . .

j: I had this weird impulse to say hi.

s: You should have.

J: It would have been weird.

P: My hands got all sweaty.

J: I hope she didn't think we wanted to rape her.

s: What the fuck?

J: It must have crossed her mind.

s: What the fuck?

J: It obviously crossed her mind.

P: Shit.

s: I looked at her.

J: Me too.

s: We shouldn't have looked at her.

J: It felt weird not to look at her.

p: Yah.

s: Well . . . I guess . . . it's late.

J: Sure, yah . . . right.

s: Brunch at eleven?

J: / Yah.

p: Right, okay.

P: Night.

J: Later.

S: Good night.

unit B-1717

À Geneviève L. Blais.
Merci de m'avoir mise au défi de plonger dans l'obscurité.

special thanks

Thank you to Geneviève L. Blais, Maryse Warda and Emma Tibaldo for your dramaturgical input and detailed work to realize this piece in both English and French simultaneously. It was no small feat! Thank you to Ainsley Hillyard, Roxanne Cote and the entire team at Theatre Yes for commissioning and producing the workshop version of *Unit B-1717* as part of the site-specific play *Anxiety*.

Unit B-1717 (*Local B-1717*) was commissioned and produced by Théâtre à corps perdus and was first produced in a storage unit facility in Montreal, from April 1 to 29, 2018, running alternately in French and English with the following cast and creative team:

French performer: Marie-Ève Milot
English performer: Laurence Dauphinais

Director: Geneviève L. Blais
Translator: Maryse Warda
Dramaturge: Emma Tibaldo
Set Design: Marie-Eve Fortier
Costume Design: Fruzsina Lanyi
Original Music: Symon Henry
Lighting Design: David-Alexandre Chabot
Technical Direction: Rébecca Brouillard
Stage Manager: Joanie Pellerin
Assistant Director: Daniel D'Amours
Technician: Stéphanie Raymond
Artistic Consultant: Eric O. Lacroix
Graphic Design: Catherine Parent

part 1

The audience enters.
The woman enters.
She heads toward the stairs.
She turns back and speaks to a surveillance camera.

I heard a . . .
scream . . .
just now
or
a couple of minutes ago, I guess,
but I'm sure I heard a scream?
Or . . .

Maybe I . . .

Probably just my . . .

Okay.
Key.
I've been forgetting my key lately.
Don't know where my brain has been
but it's my last opportunity
to have one last look so I hope that I— *(finds the key)*

Good.
That's good.

> *She heads toward the stairs.*
> *She turns back again.*

It's strange . . .
The weather this time of year.
Just when you think you can turn off the heat,
just when you think you can change your tires,
just when you think you can go out for the night without your coat
it suddenly gets so cold.
And the disappointment is palpable.
It's in the air.
In the concrete.
On the breath. *(blows out)*
Makes you wish you weren't trying to quit smoking.

> *She heads toward the stairs.*
> *Again, she stops.*

It's a ridiculous habit.
Acceptable for a mid-twentysomething
in the midst of figuring things out,
but as you approach your thirties
you really need to quit or people look at you with pity.
Or disgust.
There's that too.

That's why I only have one a night.
Wait till I'm banging my head against the wall
because I've run out of words,
or can't connect one thought to the next,
or can't remember why I'm even trying
to connect one thought to the next,

then I go for my smoke
and end up wandering . . . here.

Not that I've been working tonight.
I just . . .

Submitted my thesis today.
Yay.
Now all I have to do is wait for the critique,
for the questions that expose the research I've missed,
the arguments I've missed,
the connections I've missed;
for that inevitable sense of failure.

Lately I have this feeling of dread
whenever I get near my storage unit.
It's in the basement, so maybe that's it,
but tonight I have to go in,
need to make sure I haven't left anything important behind,
because the Diabetes Foundation is coming in the morning
to cart away anything they think they can sell,
then the junk truck will pick up the rest.

It's time.

I've had this space for way too long.

The $67.50 per month
is draining my empty bank account.

She tries to go for the stairs again.

I saw that guy again today.
The one with his laptop in the coffee shop,
the one who works there all day long.

And he's sitting at a table with an empty coffee mug,
ignoring the barista's passive-aggressive questions
about whether he'll be needing anything else,
ignoring the mother of twins who is trying to wrangle her stroller
between the back of his chair and the counter,
ignoring the group of four who want to sit
at the table of four he is occupying all by himself,
and it makes me tense just seeing him,
just watching him ignore the needs of others around him,
and instead of feeling angry like the others in the café,
I'm absorbing their anger on his behalf,
I'm taking on the shame that he's refusing to take on
and hating myself for doing it, which makes me run out the door
before I even get my coffee.

I can't work in coffee shops.
I need to work in the night.
I need the emptiness of it.
The coolness of it.
The intimacy of a single light source
suspended in a sea of darkness,
which is why I keep ending up here?
I descend to the labyrinth of corridors lined with numbered
green doors
and wander back and forth and around.
The thoughts come so clearly down there.
I imagine tucking each thought under its own door,
organizing them into chronological spaces,
and when I get back to my desk
I can write with purpose and absolute clarity.

I was taught to be scared of the night.
That women disappear at night.
Women go missing at night.
Women don't make it home when they walk alone at night,

but that assumes that all women want to appear.
That all women intend to be found.

I applied for a couple of post-docs . . .

Fuck, these shoes.

                                                    She takes them off.

Sssss. *(sizzling sound as she places her warm feet on the cold floor)*
This isn't even my skirt.
Or my top.
My friend said I needed to celebrate . . .

For most people this is just overflow:
office files, Christmas decorations,
boxes of memorabilia no one wants to sort through
and furniture, of course,
lots of furniture.
Inherited furniture from a childhood home
the owner can't bear to get rid of because that furniture
was the landscape of her youth.
She has a feeling about that furniture
so she locks it up here thinking, one day,
when she buys a house,
or a cottage up north,
there will be a use for it all.

I watch a woman come in
and I can tell she hasn't opened her locker for a while.
She lurks outside the door—
she has trouble finding her key—
and when she does go in, she has a look of pure disappointment.
Like she was expecting to find something useful,
something treasured, something that could adapt to new circumstances,

but when she sees her mother's dinette set
propped up against the rude wall of the unit,
it just looks sad,
and old,
and somewhat grotesque.
Like a homeless man in the metro,
or a drunk uncle at a wedding,
it elicits a feeling of pity and guilt
for not having dealt with it sooner.

The men come with a truck
to take everything in her unit to the dump.
I watch the surveillance screens through the window of the office,
and see each camera capture a part of the journey:
leaving the unit,
walking down the first hall,
turning into the second,
loading into the elevator,
unloading from the elevator
and passing by me standing in front of the security screens
before it gets tossed in the truck.
As the men carry each piece away:
the Persian carpet, the rocket ship toddler bed,
the dinette set,
I feel peeled back,
exposed somehow and mournful of the fate of those once-cherished,
once-lived-on objects.
I'm watching them be lugged to their execution
and I'm just standing there.
Bearing witness.
Thinking I should protest.
Thinking I should give them one last touch,
one last memory to hold onto because this is the moment reclamation
becomes no longer possible.

I suppose nothing can be useful forever.
Nothing can be endlessly treasured.
Everything eventually ends up in the dump.

When they finish emptying the unit,
I walk downstairs to have a look inside.
On the walls and the floor I can see the outline
of everything that's been removed.
The dust that had settled around the furniture over time
has left a discernable imprint
and I have the strange sensation of seeing something
that no longer exists.

In the back corner I notice a small heap,
which has been neglected by the movers.
It looks like a bunched-up sweater on the floor.
Or an armrest, perhaps,
but there's something odd about the shape of it.
Angled in parts, contoured in others.
Not fabric.
Definitely not fabric.

I reach for the light switch and discover that the single bulb has
burned out.
I should go and ask someone for a new one;
I should get the flashlight I keep in my unit,
but something about this heap will not let me turn away.
I am drawn toward it, almost without my consent,
and there is just enough light spilling in from the hall
for me to see if I get a little bit closer,
just a little bit closer, and by this point I'm curious,
what is this confounding shape?

What is that pungent smell?

I see . . .
I see . . .
I see a wing.
The bright blue wing of a small bird.
A blue jay, perhaps?
And it's perched atop what appears to be
a pile of dead birds.
There are teeth marks in their soft underbellies
but they have not been entirely devoured.
In fact, there's little trace of blood.

Wings are splayed and bent at unnatural angles.
Heads are turned too far to the right or the left.
Little claws are spread or curled around the claws of other birds.
Are they holding one another for comfort?
Are they trying to claw their way to the top of the heap?
Are they trying to be seen?
To escape?
To fly?

(hearing something) What was that?
Was that a . . .

Probably just the voices of people
rooting around in their units.

My hearing has become very acute.
Every footstep, every door slam,
every whisper is as loud as thunder.
And my sense of smell . . .
the putrid stench of a used tissue
dropped in a garbage can five blocks away . . .
And this taste . . .
I have this taste in my mouth.
The taste of a cigarette I smoked a few days ago.

I really have to quit . . .

There was screaming last week too.
I was watching the surveillance footage
when I heard it.
This terrifying scream.

On one of the screens I see these cats
—they're always getting in somehow,
I don't know how they're getting in—
but there are three tomcats surrounding one female.

They've cornered her.
Backed her up against a wall.
They're crouched and poised and leering
and creeping ever closer.
She knows she's outnumbered
but she's planning to put up a fight
and she screams:
     "Back off, assholes!"
They slowly advance,
smirking, chuckling, saying:
     "No fucking way."
She screams again and I run down the spiral stairs,
get to the bottom and rush through one corridor after the next
looking for these cats, trying to find this sound,
and I notice clumps of dirty snow in the halls.

Who dragged the end of winter inside?
Was it the cats?
Was it me?
I slow down so I don't slip,
so I don't become a puddle on the floor,
but as I'm walking I hear footsteps.
Footsteps that coincide with mine

so I can't be sure if someone else is walking
or if the sound of my own footsteps
is somehow being amplified.
It seems as though someone is walking
at the exact same pace
with the exact same weight as me.

I need to get a job.
Get out in the day.
Try to shake this sense of dread.
My hands are sweaty, but my skin is dry.
My heart is racing, but my breath is slow
and it's impossible to concentrate.
I've been losing hair,
losing weight,
losing track of time,
and the only thing that calms me down
is watching the surveillance screens,
particularly this one here.

The camera positioned outside the office
captures me watching the screens through the window,
so I, myself, am projected.
The camera is positioned above me on my right side
so I am watching a bird's-eye view of my profile.
When I watch myself like that
I get the feeling of an odd sort of unity.

The camera is taking my image from me,
the screen is taking my image from the camera,
I am taking my image from the screen
and on it goes into infinity.
Like standing between two mirrors,
watching yourself repeat until you disappear.

When I can get my mind to understand this circuit,
to fully comprehend what is happening to my image,
I feel like I'm being spun in a circle.
Like I am one point on a digit spinner
being propelled around someone's thumb and forefinger.
Or like I'm on a frantic ride in an amusement park.
Or I'm a molecule being spun apart in one of those lab machines.
And when I lock into that sensation,
when I completely understand that I'm myself watching myself
watching myself watching myself,
it's almost impossible to disengage,
almost impossible to stop watching,
and in that moment I feel completely
whole.

But lately that feeling of fullness has mutated.
Instead of feeling complete, I am full of the terror
that if I stop watching, if I step away from the circuit,
my self will get lost in the process.
That my true self will get caught in the image
and the only part of me that will survive
will be my bird's-eye profile.
How ridiculous is that . . .

I've been trying and trying to have one last look in my storage unit.
To have one last check before tomorrow
just to make sure I haven't left anything valuable behind.
To make sure there's not some secret stash of money
I don't know about taped to the bottom of my grandmother's sofa,
or a valuable antique side table my parents always thought was worthless,
or a picture of myself as a child looking confident and whole . . .

But I know . . .
I know there's nothing special about the contents of my unit.

Nothing particularly precious.
Just mostly old furniture I've been storing for years,
like the bathroom cabinet I bought for my first apartment,
the Billy bookshelf I had in my undergrad dorm room.
My father's leather armchair,
my grandmother's green sofa,
a heavy TV, an obsolete VCR,
so this really shouldn't be a big deal,
this is not any cause for anxiety,
but whenever I get to the bottom of the stairs
and walk down the hall I just . . .
I just . . .

I wish I hadn't smoked my smoke tonight.
I need a cigarette to remind me of my flesh and blood.
Need to see that I remain
even as the smoke escapes my mouth
and disappears into the night sky.

I really should check my locker,
go home and make a plan for the rest of my life.

Maybe I'll watch myself for a minute or two,
just to calm myself down.
Lock into the feeling
of watching myself watching myself watching myself . . .

She does.

Who's that?
On that screen.
A woman walking down a corridor . . .
She's walking down the corridor with one hand on the wall.
She's pushing the wall like she's trying to hold it up.

And there . . .
The back of a woman's head
as she emerges from the bottom of the stairs.
And there . . . the silhouette of a woman
rushing toward the top of the stairs,
and there's something strangely familiar
about the back of that woman's head . . .
and that silhouette . . .
and the shape of that woman pushing into the wall
as she forces herself down the hallway
toward her storage unit.

But it's not . . .
These are live cameras . . .
They can't all be images of . . .

I need to separate myself from the camera,
from the screen.
I need to run to the stairs.
I need to grip the railing and race down the stairs.
I need to get to the bottom of the stairs and run down the hall
and stop at the end of the hall that leads to my unit,
but someone is watching me.
I know that someone is watching me as I stare down the hall
that leads to my unit,
but the door to my unit is open
and I no longer have the key.
Where have I put the key?

> *The woman runs down the stairs.*
> *The audience follows.*
> *She rushes down corridors.*
> *She finally stops at the end of a corridor leading to her storage unit.*
> *The door to the unit is open.*
> *The woman is exhausted.*

Dizzy.

So dizzy.

I'm going to throw up.

I'm going to pass out.

I can't pass out.

There's not enough air,
not enough air down here.
I've used it all up so I have to keep moving,
have to keep moving or I'll smother to death
here at the end of the hall.

She puts her hand on the wall.
She looks down the corridor at her unit.
She is drawn toward it and starts to make her way down the hall.

Someone is watching.

Someone is watching me.

She gets to her unit and looks inside.

There's a darkness coming from inside.
A weight seeping out into the hall.

So much dark space,
packages of dark space,
as though the dark space has been cut up into hundreds of pieces
and they're all desperate,
all longing,
all reaching out to grab a woman's arm
and pull that woman into their lonely density.

She panics,
she struggles,
she strains,
she screams into the darkness pressing in—
she screams into the darkness—
she screams—
she—

She is drawn into the unit.
The door closes.
Each audience member uses her key to open an individual storage unit.

part 2

Each audience member is in an individual locker.
They hear the woman's voice.

I open . . .
I open . . .
I open my eyes to darkness.
I am inside
somewhere.
I am under and over and through . . .
My body is contorted into an impossible position.

I am lying down . . . partly.
Or am I standing up?
I'm tilted to the side,
or maybe I am sitting?

My right arm is sandwiched between two soft objects.
My hip is resting on the corner of something hard.
My left elbow is wet for some reason
and my right knee is pushed to the side.
It is possible my left foot is making contact with the floor
but there's no way to know for sure
because I can't tell in the darkness
which way is up or down.

My body is twisted in unnatural shapes
and I'm pressed in on all sides
like a piece of fruit in a jelly,
or a child in a collapsed snow fort,
or a spilled glass of milk that's seeping between the cracks
and stinking up the place.

The air is thick with competing smells
all vying for my attention:
damp mould,
rotting fruit,
day-old sex,
cigarettes and frustration.

My skin is itchy, my muscles ache
and I try to shift my position
but discover myself to be stuck,
so the only thing that I can do is close my eyes.

When I close my eyes I see a woman.
She is standing in front of a bathroom mirror examining herself.
Her skirt is tight, her makeup is bold
and her friend grins at her from the edge of the bathtub:

"Soooo? What d'ya think?"

The woman looks at herself with intensity,
as though she is trying to make a choice.
She could be offended by this obvious mutation of her normal
uniform:
basic jeans, loose T-shirt, ponytail, no makeup.
She's never felt comfortable in clothes that make her look
like she wants to be looked at.
The woman likes to blend.
She likes to go unnoticed.

One time a hairdresser had given the woman a fashionable haircut,
and the humiliation of leaving the salon
with her hair blown back into an approximation of conventional beauty,
a beauty she knew she could never inhabit,
made her nauseous.
Men had whistled at her.
Women had scowled.
And she knew they knew she was an imposter
in a world of fashion,
but tonight,
looking into that mirror at herself in this outfit,
she decides not to scowl.
Not to roll her eyes and wipe off the mascara.
Instead she smiles.
She laughs, even.
Out loud.
A strange sense of joy spreads over her as she realizes
that for the first time she is wearing a successful disguise.

"Let's go."

The woman lets her friend pull her out the door.
I open my eyes and find I am leaning against a bookshelf.
I am tipped, slightly.
My body is rigid,
like a ladder or an ironing board
leaning in a closet
waiting to be useful.

I feel a shelf pressed into my back.
My arms are bent at the elbows
but they too are rigid.
My muscles are frozen,
my hands are fists,
my neck is tense

and I realize I am standing
in my undergrad dorm room.

The room is dark but I can make out the stack of books on my desk,
the framed photograph of my parents,
the bulletin board of Post-it Notes of things I don't want to forget.
On the other side of the room,
I see the chaotic heaps of clothing and makeup
belonging to my roommate who's perpetually out for the night.
Not that her compulsive partying is in any way her fault.
She has abandonment issues because her father left when she was thirteen,
just at that age, right at that age when a girl needs the unconditional love of her
father to ground herself for future relationships,
which is why she now craves attention from men in positions of power,
which is why she started sleeping with her married psych professor
who's finally just told her that it really has to stop,
which is why she's been so restless,
which is why I've been excessively careful to make sure our room is a caring space,
which is why I've laid out her pyjamas neatly on her pillow.

But I'm trying not to think about my roommate.
I can see myself in my bed,
trying to calm my mind.
I've been prepping for an exam the next day
and I need to get some sleep.

I hear my roommate's key in the door.

"Shhhh!" she says as she enters the room.
"Shhhh!" a male voice repeats sarcastically.

Oh no, I see myself think,

what am I going to do?
I could roll over in bed,
or cough to make it clear I'm trying to get some sleep.
I could turn on the light and say: "I have an exam the next day."
But then what?
An awkward exit and the after-guilt
of having ruined my roommate's night?
How can I do that when I know how much trouble she's been having
getting over getting dumped.
A fumbling of giggles and dropped keys.
Shirts peeled off, jeans unzipped,
mouths slapping together, hands all over the place.

I steady my breath and calm my heartbeat,
trying to signal to them through my state of relaxation
that I am, indeed, asleep.
I project a nothingness into the darkness as if to say:
I am not here.
I do not exist.
I am lying on my side facing my roommate's bed,
and I have a sense of foreboding as they stumble themselves toward it,
but I can't roll over now.

It's dark but I can make out their shadows.
My roommate lying on her bed, propped up on her elbows
watching the man she's brought home
kneel on the floor and pleasure her.
I can't imagine having that much control over a sexual encounter.

Sex is an act of receiving,
of accepting or conceding or permitting.
Not that there isn't pleasure.
There is often pleasure, but my pleasure is a fortunate byproduct
of someone else's pleasure.

My roommate runs her fingers through his hair,
directing him to where she wants him to go,
and I have the strange sensation
of running my own fingers through someone else's hair.

Lying there, watching them move in the dark,
I start to feel my own excitement rise,
and I use every bit of control, every bit of mental strength,
to contain my breath, my heart, my hands.

Their sex is over minutes after it's begun
but I'm reeling from the effort of trying to douse myself.

I close my eyes and see the woman enter a club
that's thick with sweat and hairspray and expectation.
The woman watches other women strut by with their feathers fanned,
their coloured nails gripping coloured drinks in plastic cups.
Some women are circled in tight groups,
hollering into each other's ears,
others are clinging to the bulging arms
of slick-haired men.
The woman generally prefers places
where gender codification is less apparent,
but she's dressed like a woman tonight,
so instead of trying to figure out why each person
has decided to dress like this,
instead of looking for their missing pieces,
their hidden longings,
the latent desires,
the woman decides to take the men, the women, the club at face value
and not think about it all too much.
She decides to keep herself on the surface.
To take one moment after the next.
To enjoy each thing that comes.

Her friend passes her a shot of tequila.

"Drink 'er down!"

The woman stares at the yellowish-brown liquid.
She doesn't think.
She drinks.
It burns.
A dry lemon wedge is pushed between her teeth.

"Suck!"

The woman sucks the dry lemon.

"Drink!"

The woman drinks something red.

"Fuck yah!"

The woman drinks something fizzy
and then the woman is dancing.
She's jumping up and down
in a crowd of people who are jumping up and down
to the bass that vibrates through her body
and the woman feels nothing but joy and release.
The dancing makes her have to breathe
and it feels so good to breathe
deep and into her belly.
She feels a hand on the small of her back.
She smells the man before she sees him.
Sweat and deodorant,
Red Bull and cigarettes.
She turns to look at him and finds he is looking at her
the way she sees men look at other women.
She wraps her arm around his neck.

They move together in the mass of other people
who are moving together.
His hand moves from her hip to her ass
and the woman leaves it there.

I open my eyes to find myself well concealed.
My right knee is less inhibited
but the rest of my body is stiff
and I cannot figure out whether I'm trapped or hiding.
I am lying underneath a mint-green sofa,
staring up at the rotting wood, rusted springs and torn cloth.
Inches from my face small insects crawl in and out of holes
they have made in the wood.
They are chewing and spitting,
burrowing inside, laying eggs, no doubt,
moving, constantly moving,
dropping sawdust on my face.

I feel the weight of someone sitting on the cushion above my head
and see my eight-year-old legs
dangling over the edge of my grandmother's couch.
The air is thick with grief and flowers
and the echoes of condolences:

> "I'm sorry for your loss.
> Your grandfather was a wonderful man."

My father looks lost.
My mother looks eager to leave.
My grandmother enters with a casserole dish:

> "The bread pudding," she says.
> "No one ate the bread pudding.
> It was his favourite so I made it especially,
> but no one ate the bread pudding."

I look at the casserole dish
and its grey, mucousy content.

"I would love a piece," I hear myself say.

This draws a temporary halt to my grandmother's despair.
She looks at me with true gratefulness,
with the look that makes me feel like myself.
I am appreciated.
I am needed.
I am seen.

My grandmother spoons out a large portion and passes it to me.
The moist bread is dense and spongy,
the way I imagine a brain to look.
A dead brain, I think.
My grandfather's brain, perhaps?

Everyone watches as I take a spoonful
and slide it into my mouth.

I hold the slimy lump on my tongue
and smile with approval.
I give the thumbs-up sign, afraid that if I open my mouth
it will all come pouring out.
I bite down and imagine that a hundred maggots
are released onto my tongue,
frantically squirming,
trying to escape,
daring me to spit them back into the bowl.
I coax the writhing mass to the back of my throat
and almost gag as I swallow.
Only twelve more bites to go.

I close my eyes and see the woman in the basement of the club.
She is walking out of the toilet.

"Hey."

The man from the dance floor is standing there waiting for her.

"I used to work here."

He leads her to a door.

"After you."

And she knows this is a moment of choice.
The woman can make an excuse.
The woman can pull away.
The woman can walk upstairs and find her friend,
but there is something about this situation
that seems extremely liberating.
She doesn't know anything about this man
aside from the weight of his hand on her hip.
The colour of his hair in the flashing lights.
The shape of his chest under his black T-shirt.
And this desire, of course, that much is clear.
What he wants is incredibly simple.
Hasn't her friend been saying
that all she needs is a good fuck?
The suggestion had seemed so crass.
So vulgar and unsophisticated.
Her needs are more complex, she'd thought.
The angry spaces inside her
cannot be satiated by the thrust of a man.

But now, taking in the scent of this man
propping open the door of the dark office
in the basement of the club where he used to work,
a space that vaguely reminds her of an episode of *Law and Order: SVU*
in which women were being raped in the basement of a club,
the woman starts to wonder if her friend might be right.

If there might be something freeing
in a carnal act far from words and conversations
and trying to understand another person's deepest longings.
There is nothing hidden, thinks the woman,
in this hidden space in the basement of the club.
Everything is perfectly clear.

I open my eyes to find myself
in a heap in a beanbag chair.
My bottom is sunk so deep
I can feel the cold floor underneath.
My legs and arms are sticking up at unusual angles
like a strange flower or a wounded bird.
I can move my feet and hands but cannot pry myself out of the chair.
From where I am perched I can see my fourteen-year-old self
in the light of the TV.

I am sitting in the old leather armchair
watching *Law and Order: SVU*
as my father walks into the living room.
I automatically get out of his chair
and change the channel to the hockey game
before he even sits down.

The first time I turned on the hockey,
he looked genuinely pleased.
He saw that I'd sacrificed my own pleasure for his,
that I'd changed the channel before the detectives had discovered
who'd been raping all the women.
He'd smiled at me.
He'd winked at me.
And I was filled with purpose.
But as time went along,
and I repeated this sacrifice,
he forgot what I was doing;
that I was putting his needs ahead of my own.

So then I needed to anticipate another need.
In addition to leaving the chair and changing the channel,
I went to the kitchen to get him a beer,
and the first time I did that he smiled in surprise and said:

"How lucky am I to have a kid like you."

And that filled me.
For weeks it filled me.
But like the changing of the channel,
the beer delivery got to be expected.

He didn't even look at me when I delivered the beer.
And my mother, she started frowning.
Started rolling her eyes when I entered the kitchen
and she needed me to roll my eyes back.

"Isn't it irritating that he expects you to get it for him."

The first time I rolled my eyes in response,
she gave me a knowing smile.

"We're on the same team," that smile seemed to say.
"You understand what I have to put up with."

And that eye roll seemed to sustain her
as she made dinner and placed it neatly on the dinette set,
so the eye roll became part of my routine.

I watch myself get off the chair, change the channel,
walk into the kitchen to get the beer,
roll my eyes at my mother
and deliver the beer,
but this night my mother follows me.
She storms into the living room and starts to yell at my father:

"You just sit on your ass and expect us to do all the work."
"She likes to bring me beer."
"She hates to bring you beer."
"Tell her you like to bring me beer."
"Tell him you hate to bring him beer."

I don't know what to say.
I really don't know what to say.
But their anger is focused on me.

The man's face is rough on the woman's mouth
and his hands are making their way under her shirt.

"Is this okay?"

The woman pulls his T-shirt over his head.
Her eyes have adjusted to the darkness,
and the crack of light under the door
makes it bright enough for her to see the bulge of his arms,
the hair on his chest.

She has the strange sensation of being whole.
Not divided.
No inner voice.
She isn't trying to anticipate this man's desires,
because she knows his desires,
his singular desire,
and she is determined that he will understand hers.

"Is this good?"

He slips his hand into her underwear.

The woman tells him to take his time, then hurry up.
To touch her softly, then be assertive.
She directs his tongue, his hands, his muscles, his breath, his blood,

and she has the distinct feeling of commanding her own pleasure
and is loving the feeling of commanding her own pleasure,
not caring at all about the pleasure of anyone else until:

"Oh shit."

His muscles pull away and she feels a crack inside herself.

"Fuck, I'm sorry."

His breath pulls away and the crack opens wider.
She grabs his biceps and tries to return him to the moment,
tries to pull him back to the place she felt whole.

"It's these fucking meds I'm on."

And a chasm of dread opens up in the woman.
A swell of empathy surges out and into the room
and there's nothing she can do to stop it.
She knows he's embarrassed and disappointed and humiliated
and needs for her to make it better,
needs for her to find a way to excuse his vulnerability,
and she tries to force the chasm closed,
tries not to know he needs her to tell him
it happens all the time,
he's not alone in his incompetence,
it's a normal side effect of, what is it, Prozac?
She's known lots of men on Prozac
and there are other options, actually,
other drugs he could try for depression? Is that it?
Or anxiety? Everyone's suffering from anxiety in one way or another,
he's really not alone,
he shouldn't feel like he's alone,
but the woman doesn't say all this because she doesn't want to comfort,
she doesn't want to reassure or excuse or calm or soothe or rescue the
broken parts in him and put them back together because there's no

more room inside her, no more room for anything else or anyone else so she fights to hold it back, fights to hold it all in until a sound comes from the woman, from deep inside the woman where her packages of darkness are neatly stacked away, and it's a cracking sound, a snapping sound, a bursting sound as her body is punctured from the inside and beams of light shoot out through her skin, illuminating the dirty basement and the broken man in his underwear and her body starts to tremor, her body starts to convulse as bits of her forgotten anger shoot out into the room, throwing the man back with the force of everything inside of her that's flooding into the room with a terrifying scream of rage.

Objects dissolve before her eyes: the desk, the chair, the man, the clothes, the room, the toilet, the club, the street, the city, the earth, until the woman is surrounded by darkness—she's running in darkness, searching in darkness, and I open my eyes in the darkness.

You open my eyes and you are standing in the centre of a room.
You stretch out your arms and touch . . . nothing.
You move your head and feel . . . nothing.
You move your legs and—where are your shoes?
You become aware of the door in front of you
with a crack of light seeping in underneath;
light that leads out to a hall.
A hall that leads out to a staircase.
A staircase that leads up to a series of screens that no one is watching.
It occurs to you to open the door.
I think you can open the door.
You're going to open the door.
Open the door.

and then there was you

For mothers and their children.

special thanks

Thank you Tara Rosling for choosing this piece for the Secret Theatre.

Thanks also to Maev Beaty and Alan Dilworth for an early workshop of the piece.

And then there was you was first performed at the Shaw Festival in 2018 as part of the Secret Theatre. It was directed by Tara Rosling with the following cast:

Elodie Gillett
Pamela Mala Sinha
Emily Lukasik
Gabriella Sundar Singh
Tara Rosling

and then there was you

A woman.

I see you pass by like a fish underwater
and I know a foot when I see a foot but not because I see it,
because I feel it move,
you move,
independent,
but not separate
from me.

And I know you're coming soon and I'm excited to see you,
to hold you to my breast and watch you suck
and feel you suck, but you're still inside me,
I have exclusive access,
so I'm the only one to feel you, know you, feed you,
and I don't think I'm ready to give that up.
I dream of carrying you off by the scruff of your neck
the moment you're born in blood and water
and dragging you off to a cave, somewhere,
licking you clean and burying myself in your smell,
committing my smell to your memory
so you'll never love anyone more than me.

I lie down early at night just to feel you wake up
and I try to read in bed but you're so excited to move
and when I'm still you have room and desire to test the limits
of the small world you inhabit with expert facility.
I can't stop watching the skin on my belly stretch and morph
and ripple to contain your enthusiasm,
your eagerness to explore.
You think you know how the world will stay,
how things will always be.
And I'm sad to know the truth.

You do sense there's someone else,
if not someone, then something.
Whatever it is, it's an extension of yourself,
of your body, and it rocks and rests,
rocks and rests and the cord from your belly
attaching you to the wall of this vessel
is something pleasant to wrap your little fingers around,
but it's getting cramped in this place
and your head has been stuck in something firm
for quite a while now and when the rocking starts up
you're upside down, which you've become accustomed to,
but if things keep going at this rate,
if the space around you keeps diminishing at this rapid rate,
you won't be able to move, and you've also noticed
when you press out, something presses back.
Or taps your knee or your bottom,
and there's something about that press or tap
that gives you this strange idea that there is something else,
something beyond this warm fluid, this gripping cord,
this rocking and resting.

You try to turn your head.
You nuzzle it back and forth.
Something is thinning above you.
There might be room above.

There is a definite squeezing in intervals now,
a squeezing and resting,
squeezing and resting, which is not quite as safe
as the rocking and resting, so something about that squeezing
compels you to straighten your legs,
to press out, to kick and move your head back and forth,
and your face is pressed in for a moment
and you feel, you distinctly feel, a cool sensation on the top of your head,
a sensation you've never felt before,
and something pokes your head
as you rock back inside
and you don't want to leave
so you decide to stay
and there's a resting until the squeezing starts again
and you have to push with your legs to make it stop,
this squeezing, this pressure on your face,
on the back of your head and the chill on your head,
you can feel it again, then you slide back in,
but now you know there's nothing for it,
the squeezing starts again and you push with your legs
and you push and you kick and the squeeze on your face
on your head on your shoulders and you strain
and push and straighten and slide out into
the crass chill of the wilderness.

We're out in the garden and I'm pulling up weeds
and you're shovelling rocks into your bucket.
They aren't very big rocks.
They are the rocks, the gravel, that will go underneath the deck,
when we have enough money to build a deck,
but for now they're a pile of rocks
and you're scooping them up
and putting them in your bucket

and we're having a lovely afternoon
and I get down beside you and commend your
ability to shovel rocks into the bucket:

"They are nice rocks.
Very nice rocks.
And you can play with the rocks for as long as you like.
But you are not allowed to put the rocks in your mouth.
That is the only thing you are not allowed to do.
No rocks in mouths.
It's bad.
If you put a rock in your mouth, we are going inside
for the rest of the afternoon.
That's it.
Do you understand?"

You smile.
You nod.
I know you understand.
You don't have many words yet
but I know you understand this instruction
because I use clear language
and look you in the eye
and you nod your head
and so I go back to pulling weeds,
and you go back to your rocks,
but I can see you thinking.
You're thinking about this idea
I have just planted in your head
and you weren't even thinking about putting rocks in your mouth
but now that this idea of putting rocks in your mouth has been articulated
you can't stop thinking about what it would feel like
to slip a rock into your mouth.
You touch the smooth grey surface of a rock with your finger
and imagine that finger is your tongue
sliding over the contours of the cool mass.

You touch a jagged bit and imagine it rough on the inside of your cheek.
You touch a dirty bit and imagine the grit between your
recently emerged molars.

You could do it just for a moment,
turn your back to me and pop it in
then spit it out again,
just to see,
just to know the feeling of a rock on the tongue,
but you know you shouldn't.
You know you've been told,
so you dig up some more rocks
and put them in the bucket, but you can't stop thinking about it,
you can't stop wanting it,
and now it's in your hand:
a beautiful, little, exquisite rock,
divine in structure and size,
perfect in weight and likeness to yourself,
solid, yet small, diminutive to the larger context,
to this sea of stones, so what would one rock really do,
really be in the passing of one afternoon in the garden.

Without even looking to see if I'm looking,
you pop the rock into your mouth.

I'd been waiting for you to do it
and my fingers pluck the offending object from your mouth
before you have time to know it's there
and you're scooped up and brought inside
and when you know,
when you understand what has just happened,
you are furious.
You throw yourself back,
nearly launching yourself from my arms
and I put you on the floor in the kitchen and say:

"I told you not to put rocks in your mouth.
I told you we would go inside."

And you scream and kick and go red in the face
and I feel your sadness like it is my own
and it is my own because I wanted to spend the day in the garden
but there are few things more dangerous
than a rock in the mouth
so I did what I had to do.
I connected one thing to the other.
Action, reaction.
Defiance, punishment and this is an important lesson.
One that must be taught.
By me.

It's your first swimming lesson.
You are eager and put on your boots without being asked
and wait by the door until it's time to go.
And I talk about how fun it will be,
that your teacher will ask you to do certain things
and you must try to do what your teacher asks
because he or she is your teacher
and you should always try your best to respond
to people with authority.

I consider tempering this instruction,
consider mentioning that if people in positions of power
are not acting responsibly,
if you don't agree with a rule or a law,
it's within your rights to speak out.
In fact, it's your responsibility
to demand fairness and justice at all times.
And then, of course, there are those that would abuse their authority

to satisfy personal perversions
and you should never do anything you are uncomfortable doing
and if something feels wrong it probably is
and I will always pick you up from school
so don't get into anyone's car,
even if that person is vaguely familiar,
because awful things happen to children who get into cars
or walk out of malls with strangers or people who are somewhat familiar
so we should probably think of a safe word.

I look at you standing in your ladybug rain boots,
cradling your new swimsuit and I decide to let that
intrusion on naïveté wait for another day or week or month, even.
There are very few circumstances one of us isn't with you,
so let's keep today about swim lessons and swim instructors
and I'll be watching through the observation window of the pool
to see that you're trying your best.

And we're out on the deck with three other children
and their respective caregivers
and when the swim teacher calls your name,
you march right over, smiling, and say:
"That's me."
She smiles back with not quite enough kindness,
not quite enough reassurance for the first day of swim class,
but you're proud of yourself and you look back at me
so openly vulnerable and trusting.

The swim teacher, who hasn't told you her name,
slips into the pool and asks the four of you
to sit on the steps that lead into the water.
One boy clings to his mother, whining and whimpering
and refuses to get in the pool.
The swim teacher tries to coax him in,
but he refuses to let go of his mother.
The teacher starts the class.

You smile and wave at me from where you sit on the step.
I swell with pride because you're doing what I've asked you to do.
You're trying everything.

You put your ear in the water.
You put your chin in the water.
You put your nose in the water.
You put your whole face in the water
and I've never seen you do that before.
You've never done that with me.
You sputter and gasp as you lift out your face.
You wipe the water from your eyes and your nose.
The water, it seems, fills every space you give it.
It moves quickly, infiltrating every hole
and the bath is different than this pool.
The bath is warm and contained,
but this, this is different.
It's a large, vast space and a woman whose name
you don't even know is the only one preventing you
from filling up with water.

And now this instructor has taken you under the arms.
She has flipped you on your back
and holds you to the surface with your hair splayed around your head
and asks you to spread your arms and your legs like a star.
"Be a star," she says. "Be a star."
So you do.
You try.
But your little feet pop out of the water.
She pushes them gently down
and tells you to take in a breath.
You obey and she lets you go.
My heart stops.
She picks you up as quickly as she'd let you go
and commends your effort:
"Good job. You did it. You did a float."

She doesn't acknowledge the fear and panic on your face,
in your body.
You cling to this teacher because you no longer trust her
and I'm the one who told you to trust her.
You look at me and I cheer a silent cheer:
"Good job! You did it! Way to go!"
You steal confidence from my confidence
though you suspect I'm just as suspicious of this woman
as you are.
You see my fear.
You see my panic.
You know I'm thinking if I look away
that woman will let you drown.
You smile to reassure me that would never happen
and I steal confidence from yours.

At the end of the class I wrap your shivering body in a towel.
I tell you how impressed I am
seeing you dunk your head in the water
and float on your back
and wasn't that teacher nice
and next time we'll ask her her name.

"Next time?" you ask with suspicion.
"Next week, yes. There are nine more classes."
"I don't want to do it again."

That's all you say but next week you cry and sob.
You don't want to do it again.
You can't, you won't, you'll miss me too much
when you're in the pool and you grab onto my leg
and you struggle as I force you into your swimsuit
and into the shower and I get myself wet
making you do the obligatory rinse.
I take you out onto the deck,
make eye contact with the teacher

and put you down onto the wet tiles.
I go back into the change room
and close the door.
I stand behind it listening to you scream for ten seconds,
twenty seconds,
thirty seconds,
then quiet.

There is a cat that hangs around our house.
It's an orange cat so we call it the Orangey Cat
and say hi when we pass it,
"Hi, Orangey Cat."
We don't know who owns it
but it's a particularly precocious cat.
When I leave the doors open to bring things in or out,
like groceries, for example,
the stupid thing sneaks in the door of the house or the car
or the garage and I don't notice until
I have everything unpacked and I look at the couch
and he's sitting there curled up on my favourite blanket
and I yell at him,
"Get out of here!"
I usually lunge at him, arms flailing,
and once I even kicked him
—not on purpose, you understand,
I only wanted him to think I was going to kick him,
but then I did, not too hard, but I kicked him.
Still, he's not deterred.

It's not that I hate animals.
Just cats.
I'm allergic to cats.
Especially this orangey cat.

And this particular day
I find him up in my room lounging on my pillow
and I yell and swear and swat in his general direction
until he leaps onto the wardrobe, knocking the photographs to the floor,
the ones in the expensive frames,
and the glass smashes and I swear again
and grab the cat and it takes every bit of compassion I can muster
not to wring its little neck
and kick it through the front door like a football
and then I turn to see you standing in the doorway.

"This cat!" I yell, "I hate this cat!"
And you shake your head slowly.
"I don't," you say. "I like this cat.
You shouldn't be mean to the Orangey Cat."
"This cat is mean to me!"
"Cats can't be mean. Look."
And the repulsive thing is rubbing its head on my chest.

You take the cat from my arms with a strange sort of confidence—
have you even held a cat before?—
and you leave me standing in a pool of broken glass.

You spend hours on the porch playing with the Orangey Cat.
You stroke it, you talk to it, you save up your allowance to buy it treats,
and when I finally agree, on a cold winter night,
to let the cat stay in your room,
you look at me with a gratitude I haven't seen in a while
and for a moment I'm glad for the Orangey Cat.

The cat stays the winter but goes out in the spring.
He returns most mornings with an offering:
a mouse, a bird, occasionally a rat.
I see you cleaning the mess from the porch
before I see it's there.

Then one day the Orangey Cat doesn't come back.
I'm glad but you're not so I try to contain my relief—
no more hair on my pillow,
no more death by the door,
no more whispered confessionals to that cat on the porch.

How long can you look out the window, I wonder,
how long can you dwell in longing and expectation.
Like an unrequited lover
waiting for a sign
you linger by the window.
And when I see your hope giving way to despair,
it bothers me.
It's just a stupid cat.

I try to distract you with board games
and movie nights but a part of you is always
pining for that cat.
That Orangey Cat that isn't even ours.

So one night, after dinner, when you're looking out the window,
I decide longing should give way to grief:

"You have to let him go. He's probably dead by now."
"What?"
"These street cats face all sorts of dangers.
Raccoons.
Cars.
He could have fallen from a roof."

Your body swells with emotion.
Your face turns red and tears burst from your eyes.
I open my arms to take your grief.
To welcome a release of pain.
To comfort you.

"You're glad.
You hated him.
You always wished he was dead."

You storm from the room.

I turn on the television.

Then one day I need to repad the chairs in the dining room
and I go to the garage to get the pads—
I seem to remember putting them in the tool box,
or maybe they're in the bin at the back.
The smell stops me where I stand.
The patio umbrella is torn to shreds,
my garden tools are upturned
and there he is.
Curled up on my old office chair.
Lifelike, but still.

It's my birthday and we are having friends to the house
and you've always been so sweet on my birthday.
You picked me a bouquet of weeds one year,
painted a mural the next
and last year you even made me dinner.

But this year is the year I turn one of those ages
I've always considered to be,
we've all considered to be,
really old,
so rather than get caught up in nostalgia or regret
we decide to have a party
with friends and a caterer out in the back garden.

As we're getting ready,
as the guests are about to arrive,
you ask me if it would be all right if you go to see a friend
a little later on.
Not right away, but a little later on,
when things have simmered down.
After the cake, maybe?
I tell you I was hoping you'd be there all night,
that you're the most important guest,
that we always spend my birthday together,
and you nod and say okay,
it's just your friend is having a rough time,
and only lives a few blocks away,
just past the park and you'd be right back;
you just feel you should be there for your friend.

And I ask you which friend?
Do I know this friend?
And where exactly does this friend live?
And what's the problem with this friend anyway?

But you don't like questions anymore,
so you say, "Never mind, forget I asked,"
and slump away into the kitchen,
leaving me with the murky discomfort
of feeling like I'm the bad guy,
like I'm somehow being unreasonable,
like I'm punishing you by making you stay here for my birthday,
and I'm mad at you for making me feel this way
but I'm not just going to give in and say
"go ahead" and pretend it doesn't matter
because you have a responsibility to me above everyone else,
and one day you'll look back on this evening
and be glad you spent it with me.

The night progresses as I expect the night to progress
and the garden looks lovely with the solar-powered fairy lights
and the Middle Eastern–inspired spread
and everyone comments on my new haircut,
commends me for deciding not to dye out the grey.
"I've earned every one of these!" I laugh,
and drink another glass of pinot grigio.

But in every minute of every conversation
I'm thinking about you and watching you
out of the corner of my eye.
I see you talking to one of the family friends
we used to go on holiday with
and you're giving an update
about school and soccer and where you see yourself
studying in a year or two when you graduate.
But your hand is in your pocket on your phone
and every now and then,
between conversations you clearly wish you weren't having,
you turn away to text someone—the friend, presumably,
and I can see you want to go,
I can see you think you need to go,
and I'm mad at myself for feeling guilty at having trapped you here.
I'm making you stay because you have a responsibility to stay,
because you need to know you don't always get what you want in
this world
and because I don't want you to go.
I want you to be here.
I want you to want to be here.
I want you to need me and know that you need me.
I want you to laugh with me or cry in my arms and tell me your secrets
and lie on my bed with your head on my shoulder
and know that I know you more than anyone knows you
because I made you and guided you toward the person you are,
the person of compassion and kindness and intelligence

and fairness and good taste with a hunger for adventure
and travel and cultural experiences and a little bit of mischief.

"Happy birthday to you.
Happy birthday to you."

They start to sing and carry out the cake.
It's a lovely cake.
A truly beautiful cake.
A chocolate cake.
My favourite kind of cake.
And I smile.
I blow out the candles.
Everyone cheers.
I look up to see if your misery has finally become an apology.
But you're not where you were a moment ago;
you're not by the table or the door to the kitchen;
you're not on the deck or out on the lawn,
not by the shed or the gate leading into the alley.
You're no longer in the garden.

Did you leave?
Did you go?

And then you were gone.

First edition: December 2020
Printed and bound in Canada by Rapido Books, Montreal

Jacket design by Kisscut Design
Jacket art © Art Furnace / Shutterstock.com

 **PLAYWRIGHTS
CANADA PRESS**
202-269 Richmond St. W.
Toronto, ON
M5V 1X1

416.703.0013
info@playwrightscanada.com
www.playwrightscanada.com
@playcanpress

Erin Shields is a Montreal-based playwright. Her adaptation of *Paradise Lost* premiered at the Stratford Festival and won the Quebec Writers' Federation Playwriting Prize, and her play *If We Were Birds*, which premiered at Tarragon Theatre, won the 2011 Governor General's Literary Award. Other theatre credits include *Piaf/Dietrich* (Mirvish Productions/Segal Centre), *The Lady from the Sea* (Shaw Festival), *The Millennial Malcontent* and *Soliciting Temptation* (Tarragon Theatre) and *Instant* (Geordie Theatre). Upcoming projects include *Queen Goneril* for Soulpepper, *Jane Eyre* for the Citadel Theatre and *Ransacking Troy* for the Stratford Festival.